CW01617597

Publishers:
Alfa d.d. Nova Ves 23 a Zagreb
Podravka d.d. Koprivnica

For the Publishers:
Miro Petric
Branko Osrečki

Editors:
Ivanka Biluš
Cirila Rodé
Božica Brkan

Food Preparation, Settings:
Ljiljana Šprem
Marija Bobuš
Gordana Maričić

Food Photography:
Davor Marjanović

English Translation:
Dunja Knebl

Language Editing:
Nina H. Antoljak

Design:
Studio Piktogram

Printing:
Zrinski d.d. Čakovec
Printed in 3000 copies

Ivanka Biluš, Cirila Rodé, Božica Brkan

Cooking Around the World with Vegeta

ALFA

1999.

Electrolux
INTELLIGENT SOLUTIONS FROM SWEDEN

Electrolux is the world's largest producer of home appliances with an annual output of about 60 million units manufactured on some 20 production lines. These are products that make our lives more simple, and include: appliances for food preparation and storage, laundry and dish washing machines, water purifiers, small home appliances, industrial cleaning equipment and fitted equipment for ships and factories. As one of the leading home appliance producers Electrolux constantly works on making its products easier to work with. Our goal is to improve technology in order to solve everyday problems. A good example are our refrigerators, washing machines and vacuum cleaners. Electrolux refrigerators are the first on the market to have wheels, making cleaning under them easier. We were also the first to introduce automatic door closing and alarms to warn when refrigerator doors are not properly closed. As to vacuum cleaners, Electrolux was the first manufacturer to introduce filters, recognizing the alarming rise of illnesses due to allergies, and to asthma. The first filter made from Gore-Tex material was recently built into our appliances in co-operation with Gore Industries. The Electrolux concern has plants in more than 60 countries, all over the world. The head office of our corporation is in Stockholm, and the market is monitored from there with the participation of our Swedish investors. However, sales in Sweden amount to only 8% of our total sales. This proves that we really are an international company.

Many customers buy our products, not realizing that Electrolux backs them. There are, for example, three European white goods and kitchen appliances brands: Electrolux, AEG and Zanussi. They cover central, northern and eastern Europe. We also appear under the names Flymo, Husquarna, Volta, Gibson, White Westinghouse, Frigidaire, and others. We continue to use these brand names because of customer loyalty to them.

Electrolux is the No. 1 company in the world in energy-saving and environmentally sensitive appliances (which require less detergent to do a job well).

The "Food Care" concept was introduced in 1997 in conjunction with the Euroteque organization, which brings together more than 2,000 of the best cooks from all over Europe. In this way, we stress the advantages of Electrolux home appliances in the preparation and storage of food. For many decades now, we have been developing technologies intended to make cooking and the preservation of food more simple and effective, retaining the tradition of preparing fresh, high-quality food.

Electrolux ranks as one of the 100 strongest privately-owned enterprises in the world with more than 112,000 employees. Our goal is to be the largest or second in the world in two or three production lines.

Dear Friends!

Welcome to Vegeta's kitchen, inspired by the most famous product from the Podravka production line. This warm culinary institution is always open to our customers. It helps you to express the best of your talents as a chef, and ensures the diversity needed for real enjoyment of food preparation and good food, with practicability as the foundation of unlimited creativity.

We have been collecting recipes at the Podravka Culinary Center for almost thirty years now, and testing them by including Vegeta among the ingredients. Only the very best is presented to consumers. Cooking with Vegeta has produced an original culinary treasure-trove with hundreds and hundreds of tested recipes from the most diverse cuisines - modern and traditional, domestic and aristocratic, national and international, "fast" and "slow" ...

Vegeta recipes have been published in many books and magazines, and have also been presented for more than a quarter of a century in the popular TV series "Great Chefs' Small Secrets", where the participants are eminent cooks, chefs from almost all over the world, and famous personalities from the world of arts, show business and sport, as well as hitherto unknown masters of good cooking.

"Vegeta Recipes" is made up of the most recent team selection of great recipes created on the basis of experience gained by the Vegeta cooking team in their travels to various cities and countries. The recipes were all tested later at the Podravka Culinary Center. This chronicle is the outcome of an incredibly exciting gastronomic journey, which most of us would be hard put to undertake under our own steam. But the fruits of it are in this book which comes into your kitchen with a refreshing range of aromas, colors and tastes.

It's all up to you whether you prepare something simple or complex, cook something that's ready in a jiffy or takes much longer, some exotic national dish or a modest vegetarian meal you will be tasting for the first time: but our hope is - whatever your choice - preparing and cooking - and eating - it will always be a pleasure. The recipes have been divided into five groups, depending on the basic ingredients used: pastry, rice, dumplings, pizza, pancakes; vegetables dishes; mushroom and egg dishes; meat dishes (chicken, turkey, veal, beef, pork, lamb, wild game); and, fish dishes. Each group gives you a choice ranging from the very simple to the completely bizarre, from very famous specialties interpreted in our Vegeta way, to completely original dishes. In all cases, all the dishes are prepared with the addition of Vegeta, because numerous tastings and discussions with experts and gourmets, have convinced us once again - Everything Tastes Better With Vegeta!

We hope that this journey with us through Vegeta's cuisine will be a memorable and very tasty experience for all our readers!

Bon appetit!

Microwaves, just like light, are a type of electromagnetic energy. Under their influence water molecules in food move. The water movement inside the cells produces the heat for heating food. Microwave ovens are perfect for defrosting and heating food.
Electrolux microwave ovens also have a powerful quartz grill. During the process of defrosting, the Electrolux microwave oven will determine by itself the time needed for certain type of food to defrost completely, and this depends on the weight.
Note:
When preparing food in a microwave oven, use only dishes made of porcelain, ceramics, glass or paper. If a dish has thicker walls, more time will be needed to cook or defrost.

pasta, rice, dumplings, pizzas, pancakes...

pasta, rice, dumplings; pizzas, pancakes...

Characteristic aromatic herbs play a very significant role in Mediterranean cuisine, and basil leaves are the final touch to the following dish. It is made tastier by the addition of olive oil, grated cheese and garlic. Pestle or pesto in Italian is made in various different ways and Vegeta's cooking team had the opportunity to taste it in Genoa. Most often it is used with pasta.

Pasta with Basil Leaves

(serves 4)

Ingredients:
400 g/ 14 oz pasta
200 g/ 7 oz hulled peas
20 g/ 1 oz dry-smoked bacon
4 tablespoons olive oil
2 cloves garlic
basil leaves
3 tablespoons Parmesan cheese
salt, pepper
lemon juice
200 ml/7 fl oz cream
1 teaspoon Vegeta

Dice the bacon finely. Prepare the basil leaves mixture: crush the garlic cloves, add the basil leaves, grated Parmesan cheese, olive oil and pepper. Mix the ingredients well.

Cook the pasta in salted boiling water. Fry the diced bacon in a small quantity of oil in a large saucepan, add the peas and Vegeta. Braise adding a little water from time to time until the peas become tender, then add some lemon juice. Add the cooked drained pasta to the prepared peas as well as the basil leaf mixture. Mix well and heat a little adding the water leftover from cooking the pasta, the cream and the chopped parsley.

Note: The pasta will be more savoury if you add a little of the liquid leftover after cooking pasta to the sauce.

Preparation and cooking time: about 30 minutes
(1 serving amounts to 661/2779 Cal/J)

Macaroni with Rocket Leaves

(serves 4)

The Ligurian cuisine was presented to the Vegeta cooking team with a pasta dish made of macaroni with rocket leaves. Rocket has been known from the Roman times and is a favorite in the modern Italian cuisine. Rocket grows wild and its young leaves are a favourite as a salad in the whole Mediterranean region, and the Adriatic zone as well. Why not try a new recipe?

Ingredients:

350 g/ 11 1/2 oz macaroni
2-3 cloves garlic
120 g/4 oz rocket leaves
300 g/ 10 oz aubergines
30 g/ 1 oz pine nuts
50 g/ 2 oz black olives
salt, pepper
20 g/ 1 oz butter
3 tablespoons olive oil
50 g/ 2 oz grated semi-hard sheep cheese or Parmesan cheese
1 teaspoon Vegeta

Cook the macaroni (the short ones called penne rigate) in salted water "al dente" which means that they should not be overcooked. Drain them and keep part of the liquid they had been cooked in.

Peel the aubergines, sprinkle with salt and leave aside to rest shortly. Drain them on paper towels.

Fry the previously diced aubergines in preheated butter in a saucepan. Add crushed garlic, pepper, chopped olives and Vegeta. Then add the cooked maca-roni, part of the liquid they have been cooked in, olive oil and part of the pine nuts, previously fried.

Cook shortly and when almost done add coarsely chopped rocket leaves, grated cheese, mix well and serve after having sprinkled with the remaining pine nuts.

Preparation and cooking time: about 25 minutes
(1 serving amounts to 527/2205 Cal/J)

Although Italian cuisine has become popular the world over, there is no end of new ways how to prepare the always popular pasta. Olive oil, pancetta (cured and dried bacon) and the ubiquitous tomatoes, as well as many other seasonings, as for instance rocket leaves in the following recipe make the dish tastier in a new way and prove that there is no end to creating new combinations.

Pasta Shells with Rocket Leaves

(serves 4)

Ingredients:
400 g/ 14 oz pasta - shells or fusilli
2 tablespoons olive oil
20 g/ 1 oz onion
150 g/5 oz cured bacon (streaky)
100 ml / 4 fl oz white wine
250 g/ 9 oz tomato
salt, pepper
1 hot chilli pepper
1 aubergine
100 g/ 4 oz rocket leaves
100 g/ 4 oz sheep cheese
1 teaspoon Vegeta

Cut the bacon into thin strips and chop the onion finely. Peel the aubergine, dice it, roll in flour, fry in a small quantity of oil and remove when done. Cut the washed rocket leaves into wide strips.

Cook the pasta in a large quantity of salted boiling water. Fry the onion and bacon in olive oil, pour over with wine and leave to cook. Add the tomatoes, Vegeta, freshly ground pepper, a pinch of salt and chopped chilli pepper. Mix and cook until the liquid evaporates. Add the fried aubergines, cooked and drained pasta as well as a small quantity of water left-over from cooking the pasta. Add the rocket leaves and mix well. Place in a serving bowl and sprinkle with grated sheep cheese.

Note:
You can use green radicchio instead of rocket leaves.

Preparation and cooking time: about 35 minutes
(1 serving amounts to 881/3684 Cal/J)

Spaghetti with Tuna

(serves 4)

The following simple and fast-to-prepare dish is a famous Italian specialty, and its characteristic taste is popular all over the world. Although the general opinion is that the main secret of tastiness lies in the sauces with interesting combinations so that instead of basil leaves one may use origano, it is also possible to create surprises by using different kinds of pasta, and choosing, for instance macaroni, broad noodles, or shell pasta instead of spaghetti.

Ingredients:

400 g/14 oz spaghetti
1 can tuna
100 ml / 4 fl oz oil (sunflower and olive oil mixture)
2 cloves garlic
1 can diced tomatoes "Podravka" (440 g/1 lb)
basil leaves, parsley leaves
50 ml/3 fl oz white wine
salt
pepper
grated Parmesan cheese
1 tablespoon Vegeta

Fry the halved garlic cloves in a not too hot oil mixture until they change color slightly and remove from the saucepan. Add the chopped tomatoes and Vegeta to this oil and braise until the liquid evaporates. Add and mix in the wine, tuna pieces, basil leaves, pepper and season with salt to taste. Cook shortly and mix in the chopped parsley. Pour this sauce over the cooked and drained spaghetti and sprinkle with grated Parmesan cheese.

Preparation and cooking time: about 30 minutes
(1 serving amounts to 656/2757 Cal/J)

Emilia Romagna sailed into the waters of international cuisine thanks to fried vegetables and piadinos, mortadella, cheese, sweets, and, of course pasta, and due to the old culture of her country and its abundance of products.

The Vegeta cuisine team had great pleasure in watching the production of tortelline, tortelloni, gnocchi, canelloni, lasagne, tagliatelle made by the magic palms of the trattoria "Annamaria" in Bologna... And afterwards, could anyone resist tasting these wonderful products with a real Bolognese sauce?

Pasta with Bolognese Sauce (serves 4)

Ingredients:
400 g/ 14 oz pasta (broad noodles, macaroni, spaghetti, or gnocchi)
4 tablespoons olive oil
30 g/1 oz butter
250 g/ 9 oz minced beef
50 g/ 2 oz cured bacon
1 onion
1 carrot
20 g/ 3/4 oz celeriac - root
150 g/ 5 oz chopped tomatoes "Podravka"
1 tablespoon tomato purée
2 chicken livers
2 cloves garlic
salt
freshly ground pepper
nutmeg
origano
bay leaf
100 ml / 4 fl oz white wine
1 tablespoon Vegeta

Chop the bacon, onion and garlic finely. Grate the carrot and celeriac root. Preheat the oil and butter mixture in a saucepan with thick base. Fry the minced meat. Add the bacon, onion, carrot, celeriac root and garlic and braise shortly. Mix in the chopped tomatoes, a small amount of salt, Vegeta, and braise for about 10 minutes. Add the tomato purée, grated nutmeg, origano, bay leaf, freshly ground pepper and wine. Cook over low heat for about one hour, adding water when necessary. When almost cooked add the chopped chicken liver.

Pour the sauce over cooked pasta and serve with grated Parmesan cheese.

Preparation and cooking time:
about 1 hour and 30 minutes
(1 serving amounts to 466/1958 Cal/J)

Rice with Courgettes

(serves 4)

The Vegeta cooking team returned from Lago di Garda lake full of wonderful impressions and found inspiration in risotto, the very famous dish loved by many which is like a cult to the Italians. In Italy risotto has gained the status of an independent meal, primo piatto. Together with the very famous Milanese risotto which is yellow in color due to the use of saffron, especially favorite dishes are risotto with fruits of the sea and with vegetables, like the following very simple, light summer dish.

Ingredients:

250 g/ 9 oz rice
500 g/ 1 lb courgettes
5 tablespoons olive oil
20 g/ 3/4 oz butter
150 g/ 5 oz spring onions
3 cloves garlic
1 chicken soup cube
pepper, salt
50 ml / 2 fl oz wine
basil leaves, parsley
grated Parmesan cheese
1 tablespoon Vegeta

Peel the courgettes partly, if necessary and dice them. Clean the spring onions and slice into rings. (Use part of the green stalks as well).

Put the onions, crushed garlic and the courgettes in cold olive oil, stir and fry. Add the Vegeta and rice, braise shortly, mix in the butter, soup cube, salt, pepper and pour over 800 ml/1 1/2 pints water. Mix well and cook slowly in a covered pan. Stir the rice occasionally. When it is half tender add the wine and stir (if you wish you may add a little wine vinegar), basil leaves and chopped parsley.

Serve the risotto warm with grated Parmesan cheese.

Note:
A pan with a thick base is recommended for cooking this risotto.

Preparation and cooking time: about 25 minutes
(1 serving amounts to 473/1987 Cal/J)

Preparation and cooking time: about 45 minutes
(1 serving amounts to / 931/3910 Cal/J)

Paella Valenciana

(serves 4)

Paella is a famous Spanish dish which is cooked in a wide saucepan after which it was named, from various ingredients found on land and in the sea, but always in combination with rice.

Ingredients:

1/2 young chicken
200 m/ 7 fl oz oil
8 scampi
200 g/ 7 oz mussels
100 g/ 4 oz date shells (finger fish)
100 g/ 4 oz cuttle-fish
100 g/ 4 oz green beans
100 g/ 4 oz onion
3 - 4 cloves garlic
100 g/ 4 oz tomatoes
200 g/ 7 oz rice
100 g/ 4 oz large beans
4 artichoke hearts
2 peppers (green and red)
salt, pepper
saffron
1 tablespoon Vegeta

Cut the chicken into small pieces, clean the cuttle-fish and dice, and clean the shell-fish well. Dice the peppers, and chop the onion and garlic finely. Cut the green beans into small pieces, and cook the previously soaked beans. Fry the chicken in the preheated oil and place on a plate. Fry the onion golden in the same oil, then add the prepared peppers, garlic and diced peeled tomatoes. Add a little water and leave to braise slowly.

Add the chicken, scampi, mussels, date-shells and diced cuttle-fish, artichoke hearts, green beans, cooked beans, and saffron dissolved in water to this sauce. Season with a little salt, pepper and add the Vegeta.

When it comes to the boil add the washed rice and braise, adding water occasionally.

Potatoes with Rice

(serves 4)

The following vegetarian dish is universal and familiar to all because it can be prepared with ingredients found in any household. In summer it can be served with fresh salad, made from different kinds of vegetables and can be a very attractive, colorful and very refreshing meal.

Ingredients:

1 kg / 2 pounds potatoes
200 g/ 7 oz rice
1 onion
6 tablespoons oil
salt, pepper
parsley
1 tablespoon Vegeta

Peel the potatoes and slice thinly. Chop the onion finely. Oil an oven-proof casserole or baking tin. Arrange half of the prepared potatoes, then the washed rice, sprinkle evenly with onion, pepper, a little salt, parsley and Vegeta. Arrange the remaining potatoes on top, season with a little more salt and pour over 700 ml / 1 1/2 pints water so that all the ingredients are covered. Place to bake for about 45 minutes in a hot oven at a temperature of 200 °C / 400 °F/ gas 6, until all the liquid is absorbed.

Serve fresh salad with this simple dish.

Preparation and cooking time: about 50 minutes
(1 serving amounts to 554/2328 Cal/J)

Note:
Pay attention to the way you slice the potatoes. In order for this dish to be successful the potato slices must be thin enough so that the rice and the potato become tender at the same time and absorb the liquid.

Greek cuisine is simple, rustic and imaginative, abundant with aromatic ingredients. It has many dishes containing black and green olives, various cheeses, moussakas and dolmas, with meat or vegetarian stuffing, like the following dish presented to us by the journalist and world traveler, Pero Zlatar.

Preparation and cooking time: about 1 hour
(1 serving amounts to 424/1781 Cal/J)

Stuffed Vine Leaves (Dolmas)

(serves 4)

Ingredients:

200 g/ 7 oz young vine leaves
(fresh or canned)
150 g/ 5 oz onion
8 tablespoons oil
160 g/ 5 oz rice
2 tablespoons chopped dill
2 tablespoons chopped parsley
1/2 tablespoon chopped mint
salt, pepper
1 teaspoon sugar
20 g/ 3/4 oz butter
2 tablespoons lemon juice
1 tablespoon Vegeta

Briefly boil the fresh vine leaves (blanche), rinse with cold water and drain. If you are using canned leaves, follow the instructions.

Fry the chopped onion and rice in preheated oil, pour over one cup hot water, add the chopped seasoning herbs, salt, pepper, sugar and Vegeta.

Stir the ingredients and cook covered for about ten minutes on a low temperature, then leave to cool.

Line the bottom of the saucepan with vine leaves. Arrange the rest of the leaves so that the under side is up. Place a spoonful of the filling on each leaf. Fold in the leaf edges and roll up like a small parcel. Place the parcels in the saucepan. Sprinkle with lemon juice, melted butter and hot water (300-400 ml/ 1/2 pint - 14 fl oz).

Place a plate on the dolmas and cook slowly for about forty minutes.

Note:
You can serve the dolmas as a hot or cold hors d'oeuvres. The dolmas will be even tastier if you add some pine nuts to the stuffing.

The whole of the Tyrol, especially its southern part, is the exceptionally interesting historical, geographical, tourist and gastronomic heart of Europe. The region is partly Italian and it has the best specialties of the Italian and Austrian cuisines, which both surprise us with unexpected new tastes, harmony and contemporaenity.

The Vegeta cooking team was enthusiastic about the following dish which they tasted at the "Schwartz Adler" guest house. It started out as a traditional garnishing and advanced to the main course.

Spinach Dumplings

(serves 4)

Ingredients:

250 g one-day-old rolls
150 ml / 1/4 pint milk
3 eggs
1 onion
1 clove garlic
500 g/1 lb fresh spinach or
300 g/ 10 oz frozen spinach
20 g/ 3/4 oz butter
3 tablespoons bread crumbs
70 g/ 2 1/2 oz semi-hard
sheep cheese
salt, freshly ground pepper
nutmeg
origano
1 tablespoon Vegeta

Dice the rolls. Mix the milk and eggs and pour over the diced rolls. Leave to soak a little. Boil the cleaned and washed spinach shortly, drain well and chop finely.

Fry the chopped onion and garlic in oil until golden and then add the spinach. Add the prepared spinach to the soaked rolls along with the grated cheese, bread crumbs, salt, pepper, origano, grated nutmeg and Vegeta. Mix all the ingredients well and form balls with moistened hands.

Cook for about eight minutes in salted boiling water over a very low heat. Remove the cooked dumplings from the water with a slotted spoon and place them on a preheated plate. Sprinkle with grated cheese and melted butter. Serve as main course or hors d'oeuvres.

Note:
You can serve the dumplings with tomato sauce, with various meat dishes in sauce or combined with various vegetables.

Preparation and cooking time: about 45 minutes
(1 serving amounts to 423/1777 Cal/J)

Dumplings Cooked in Cloth Towels

(serves 4)

Branko Ognjenović is a Croatian cook with vast international experience. When he was a guest in the Vegeta Cuisine TV show he presented an old, traditional and well-known Viennese recipe. He served the following dumplings with chops and a tasty sauce made of mushrooms (beech-sticks), naming it "Viennese Nostalgia".

Ingredients:

300 g/10 oz white bread
30 g/1 oz butter
20 g/3/4 oz cured bacon
1 small onion
200 ml /7 fl oz milk
2 eggs
pepper
salt
nutmeg
parsley
1 teaspoon Vegeta

Dice the bread and fry shortly in butter. Fry separately the chopped bacon and onion, add the bread. Mix the eggs and Vegeta well and pour over the bread. Add pepper, a little salt, grated nutmeg, chopped parsley and stir lightly, leave to rest about 15 minutes. Stir well again, form a roll, wrap it in a kitchen towel sprinkled with bread crumbs (you may wrap it in aluminum foil, if you wish) and place to cook in salted boiling water. Cook over low heat for about 25 minutes. Remove from the water, unwrap and cut into slices.

If you wish you may form balls out of the bread mixture and cook them in salted boiling water.

Serve with various meat dishes in piquant and refined sauces, even with vegetable dishes.

Note: If you do not consume all the dumplings at once, here is how you can use the leftovers: make a mixture consisting of eggs, sour cream and chopped parsley. Pour over the dumplings, bake in the oven and serve with salad.

Preparation and cooking time: about 40 minutes
(1 serving amounts to 355/1493 Cal/J)

As everywhere in Bavaria, the favorites in Allgau are the excellent beer and the traditional dishes: white sausages, roast knuckles, pasta with cheese and, of course, Leberknodeln.

The secret of preparing liver dumplings was revealed to Vegeta's team by Jure Mula, an excellent cook, who has been working for years in Germany and runs the "Haus des Gastes" (City Guest House), in the picturesque tourist town of Obermeiselstein, not far from Oberstdorf.

Liver Dumplings

(serves 4 - 6)

Ingredients:

7 one-day-old rolls
(70 g/ 2 1/5 oz each)
about 300 ml / 1/2 pint
milk
3 eggs
250 g/9 oz beef liver
100 g/ 3 1/2 oz sweetbread
50 g/ 1 1/2 oz butter
1 onion
parsley
salt
pepper
marjoram
nutmeg
grated lemon rind
1 tablespoon Vegeta

Slice the rolls thinly and pour slightly salted tepid milk over them. Leave to rest shortly. Wash the liver and sweetbreads (used to make the cooked liver dumplings color more attractive), remove the skin and mince. Fry the chopped onion in butter until golden. Add all this to the rolls. Also add the mixed egg, pepper, marjoram, grated nutmeg, lemon rind, chopped parsley and Vegeta. Work out the dough well and season to taste.

Form large balls and cook for about 20-30 minutes in boiling salted water. The dumplings must be cooked over a very low heat.

You can serve the dumplings in many ways: in soup with chopped chives, with sour cabbage garnishing and mashed potatoes.

Note:
Instead of liver you can use minced meat.

Preparation and cooking time: about 40 minutes
(1 serving amounts to 273/1147 Cal/J)

Liptow Dumplings

(serves 8 - 10)

When travelling through Slovakia the Vegeta cuisine team was convinced that the Slovakians can really make fantastic dishes using butter made of cow or sheep milk, and with the highly appreciated sheep cheese - bryndza which is also an excellent hors d'oeuvres, with halushkas and pirohy. Master chef from Bratislava and author of several cook-books, Ondrej Antovsky prepared the following tasty dish.

Dough:

1 kg / 2 lbs potatoes
250 g/ 9 oz flour
50 g/ 1 2/3 oz semolina
1 egg yolk
50 g/ 1 2/3 oz butter
salt
100 g / 4 oz flour for the pastry

Filling:

350 g/12 oz soft sheep cheese
or fresh cottage cheese
1 egg yolk
pepper
dill or chives
1 teaspoon Vegeta

Cook the potatoes with their skins on. Mix together the well drained cheese, egg yolk, pepper, chopped dill or chives and Vegeta.

Peel the cooked potatoes and pass through a sieve. Add the egg yolk, salt, semolina, butter, flour and make a dough. Roll out the dough on a floured board to a thickness of 3-4 mm / 1/8 - 1/4 inch. Cut into rounds 5 cm / 2 inches in diameter, or squares, and place the cheese filling in the center of each, fold over the dough and press the edges together.

Cook the dumplings in salted boiling water for about 15 minutes.

Remove them from the water, pour over sour cream, sprinkle with chopped bacon or bread crumbs previously fried in butter.

Preparation and cooking time: about 1 hour and 20 minutes
(1 serving amounts to 363/1530 Cal/J)

Water Dumplings with Eggs

(serves 4)

Old traditional, but newly discovered dishes are often a very tasty and pleasant surprise. Especially if they are prepared in such a simple manner as the following one. Everyone in the family will love this simple tasty dish.

Ingredients:

500 g / 1 lb flour
1 small teaspoon baking powder
rolls
salt
400 ml/14 fl oz tepid water
4 tablespoons oil
1 onion
2 eggs
100 ml / 4 fl oz sour cream
4 tablespoons milk
1 small teaspoon Gussnel cornstarch
pepper
parsley leaves
1 tablespoon Vegeta

Put the flour, baking powder, salt and water into a bowl, combine well and make a smooth dough with the help of an electric blender or with a spoon. Leave the dough to rest a short while.

Spoon out the dough and cook in salted boiling water to which you have added a tablespoon of oil. Cook for about 15 minutes, drain.

Prepare an egg, sour cream, milk, cornstarch and Vegeta mixture.

Preheat the oil in a pan and fry the chopped onions, add the dumplings and heat well. Pour over the prepared egg mixture and mix until it thickens a little. Season with pepper and sprinkle with parsley. Serve these dumplings as a snack or light dinner together with a salad of your choice.

Note:
Boiled water dumplings are always an excellent garnishing with stewed meat or goulash.

Preparation and cooking time: about 30 minutes
(1 serving amounts to 637/2677 Cal/J)

Introducing us to old Istrian cuisine, two friends and excellent cooks from Rabac, Sergio Dragonja and Mario Licul unwrapped their memories, as well as their grandmother's kitchen towels, or canavazza. Just as they do when taking part so successfully in gastronomic competitions, they made a modern dish based on a traditional one, dedicating this interesting roll to the memory of their grandmothers and their fine cooking.

Grandmother's Canavazza

(serves 6)

Traditional

Ingredients:

Dough:

300 g/ 10 oz flour
3 eggs
salt

Filling:

500 g/ 1 lb minced beef
3 tablespoons olive oil
3 tablespoons sunflower oil
350 g/ 12 oz spinach
50 g/ 1 2/3 oz prosciutto
4 cloves garlic
salt, pepper
3 eggs
100 g/ 3 1/2 oz hard cheese
1 tablespoon Vegeta

Wash the spinach and boil briefly in a very small quantity of water. Drain and chop. Chop the prosciutto and garlic and grate the cheese.

Sauté the minced meat in the oil mixture. When the meat becomes tender add the spinach, prosciutto, garlic, salt, pepper and Vegeta. Braise a short while. When the mixture cools down add the eggs and cheese.

Then make a dough out of the flour, eggs, salt and a little water, a little softer than noodle dough. Roll out the dough thinly, spread the filling over it and roll into a strudel with the help of a tablecloth. Form it like a snail, place on a kitchen towel, tie a knot on top through whichyou pass a wooden spoon or long stick, so that the bundle hangs and does not touch the bottom of the cooking pan. Cook slowly in salted boiling water for about 40 - 45 minutes. Take the strudel out of the water, cut into slices and pour over tomato sauce into which you have mixed chopped basil leaves. You can serve this dish with grated Parmesan cheese.

Preparation and cooking time: about 1 hour and 30 minutes
(1 serving amounts to 649/2727 Cal/J)

The Vegeta cooking team was very enthusiastic at discovering a typical Slovenian tavern named Žolnir in the smallest Slovenian town - Kostanjevica, serving very tasty dishes made with buckwheat, a slightly forgotten, but very nutritious cereal, reintroduced by modern eating trends. You can make a buckwheat flour roll, with various fillings such as rind chips, sour cream and egg or walnuts, sour cream and seasoning or some other filling you fancy.

Note:
The flour and water ratio depends on how the flour was ground. If the flour is rough, you should use 350 g/ 12 oz flour and 600 ml/1 pint water.

Buckwheat Štrukli

(serves 6-8)

Ingredients:

500 g/1 pound fine buckwheat flour
500 ml / 16 fl oz water
salt
a small amount of white flour

For the cheese filling:

400 g/14 oz fresh cottage cheese
1 - 2 tablespoons sour cream
1 egg
salt
50 g/ 1 2/3 oz bread crumbs
50 g/ 1 2/3 oz butter
1 teaspoon Vegeta

Put the buckwheat flour into a bowl, pour over salted boiling water. Mix well and leave to chill. In the meantime prepare the filling: Mash the drained cottage cheese. Add the sour cream, mixed egg, a little salt and Vegeta and mix well.

Place the chilled dough on a floured board. Knead well, divide into two and roll out each part to a thickness of about 1/2 cm / 1/4 inch. Spread the prepared filling over the surface and sprinkle with some bread crumbs (the quantity of bread crumbs depends on the thickness of the filling). Roll the dough into two rolls - štrukli. Place them on towels which you have previously soaked in water, squeezed dry and sprinkled with bread crumbs.

Wrap the rolls gently into the towels and tie with thread. Place to cook for about 30 minutes in salted boiling water. Take them out of the water, unwrap, leave to rest a short while, cut into slices, sprinkle with bread crumbs fried in butter.

You can serve this dish as an independent meal with sour cream and salad per taste, or as side-dish with cutlets in mushroom sauce, or wild game stew, or similar.

It's a nice surprise if you sprinkle them with sugar and serve as dessert.

Preparation and cooking time:
about 1 hour 20 minutes
(1 serving amounts to 415/1744 Cal/J)

Note:
You can make small dumplings out of the remaining dough, boil them and sprinkle with bread crumbs fried in butter.

Pizza, that round-shaped piece of dough is a favorite all over the world. Pizza restaurants - pizzerias - always have Mediterranean aromas, tastes and colors, and the most famous ones, like the Naples pizza - margarita or quattro stagione are tasty little culinary pieces of art. The Vegeta cooking team could not resist the temptation to create a Vegeta pizza - large, square in shape, baked in a baking tin, pizza al metro, often made in Italian restaurants, but the team made it using Vegeta, which you can also do for the whole family or friends.

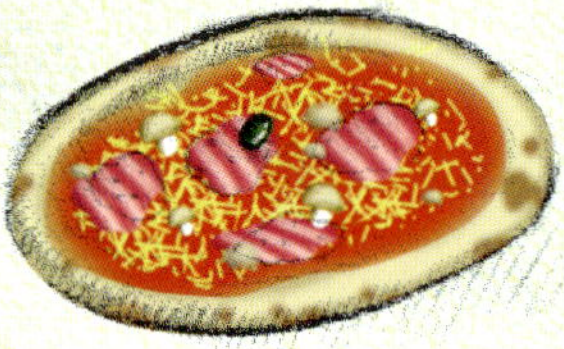

Pizza Vegeta Style

(serves 4)

Ingredients:

350 g/12 oz flour
1 sachet instant yeast (Digo)
about 200 ml/7 fl oz tepid water
salt
800 g/1 3/4 lbs chopped tomatoes
50 ml / 2 fl oz sunflower oil and olive oil mixture
150 g/ 5 oz smoked bacon
150 g/ 5 oz Gauda cheese
100 g/ 3 1/2 oz champignons - button mushrooms
salt, pepper, origano
1 teaspoon sugar
1 teaspoon Vegeta

Mix the flour with the dry instant yeast, and make a dough gradually adding tepid salted water. Place in a dusted bowl. Leave to rise until it doubles in size.

In the meantime place the chopped tomatoes in oil, add a little salt, sugar and Vegeta, and braise. Slice the bacon, roughly grind the cheese and finely slice the champignons - button mushrooms.

Spread the risen dough a little. Place in a 30 x 40cm / / 12 - 16 inch oiled baking tin, and spread it out so that it covers the whole baking tin surface raising the sides. Spread the prepared tomatoes over the dough, sprinkle with origano and ground pepper. Arrange the bacon, champignons - button mushrooms and grated cheese on top. Place the pizza into a preheated oven and bake for about 20 minutes at 200 ° C/ 400 ° F/gas 6. You can cut the baked pizza into small or large slices, triangles or thin strips.

Preparation and cooking time: about 45 minutes
(1 serving amounts to 904/3799 Cal/J)

The many interesting Turkish ethnic-dishes reminded the Vegeta cooking team that quickly prepared small portions or snacks are much older than the modern fast food. Ms Jasna Tomić from the Republic of Croatia Embassy in Ankara told us about pide, risen dough cakes with a meat, vegetable or cheese spreading, similar to the Italian pizza, the French Quiche or our Croatian pogača. To make this type of food, you do not need too much time, large quantities of ingredients nor do you need to know much about cooking. On the other hand, you can liven up the atmosphere and make your guests feel more welcome when you pass around these small portions as a surprise snack.

Pide with Cheese

(serves 4 - 8)

Ingredients:

For the dough:

500 g/1 lb flour
2 teaspoons salt
40 g/ 1 1/2 oz fresh yeast
1 teaspoon sugar
50 ml / 2 fl oz water
100 ml / 4 fl oz oil
300 ml / 1/2 pint yogurt

For the filling:

500 g/ 1 lb semi-hard cheese
2 bunches parsley
2 eggs
1 teaspoon Vegeta

Sift the flour, and leave a small quantity for making the dough. Place the flour on a board, add the salt, make a hole in the center and put into it the yeast previously mixed with sugar and tepid water. Dust with flour and leave to rise for 10 minutes.

Gradually mix in the oil and yogurt and blend well for about 7-8 minutes to make a smooth medium soft dough. Cover the dough and leave to rise in a warm place so that it doubles in size.

Place the risen dough on a slightly floured board. Divide into eight, form each piece and roll into an oval shape 1/2 cm / 1/4 inch thick. Arrange in an oiled baking tin and spread the filling over each, leaving 1 cm / 1/2 inch plain dough at the edges. Bake in the oven for about 10 minutes at a medium temperature until the pide turn golden. Serve while still hot.

For the filling: Mix the eggs with Vegeta, and pour this mixture over the roughly grated cheese. Add the chopped parsley and stir lightly.

Note
These small portions of food are quickly prepared and may be served on various occasions when you have people around.

Preparation and cooking time: about 40 minutes
(1 serving amounts to 757/3183 Cal/J)

Pancakes with Meat Filling

(serves 4)

It is not widely known that pancakes are of Hungarian origin. Some provinces, such as for instance Hortobagy, have specialties with pancakes. Pancakes are tasty and a favorite in many parts of the world. They are quickly prepared and may be served on any occasion.

Ingredients:

8 pancakes
400 g/ 14 oz roughly minced beef
4 tablespoons oil
1 onion
2 cloves garlic
salt
powdered red paprika
1 green pepper
100 g / 3 1/2 oz tomatoes
150 g / 5 oz flour
150 ml / 1/4 pint sour cream
200 ml / 7 fl oz cream
1 tablespoon Vegeta

Fry the onion in a pan in preheated oil. Add the minced meat, fry well, add the powdered red paprika and continue braising, occasionally adding water when necessary. Add the finely diced green paprika and peeled tomato, chopped garlic, a pinch of salt and Vegeta.

Finally add the flour previously mixed with two tablespoons of sour cream, cook shortly and cool a little. Fill the hot pancakes with this sauce, fold.

Use the same pan for heating the cream and the remaining sour cream. Pour part of this mixture into an oven-proof casserole. Arrange the prepared pancakes and pour over the remaining mixture. Place in a preheated oven to bake shortly, decorate with pepper pieces and serve while still hot.

Preparation and cooking time: about 1 hour
(1 serving amounts to 605/2544 Cal/J)

Pancakes "Mandriera"

(serves 4)

The following pancakes are a specialty of the famous Trieste restaurant "Suban 1865", and were awarded the Golden Medal at the Venice "Fogher d'oro '72", proof that pancakes can also be a festive and exceptional dish. They were prepared for the Vegeta cooking team by Mario Suban, the restaurant-owner himself.

Ingredients:

For the batter:

100 g/ 4 oz flour
1/4 l/ 8 fl oz milk
1 egg
2 egg yolks
20 g/ 3/4 oz butter
salt

Filling:

4 tablespoons olive oil
1 clove garlic
basil leaves
40 g/ 1 1/2 oz grated Parmesan cheese
pepper

Topping:

30 g/ 1 oz butter
100 ml / 4 fl oz cream
juices from meat roasting
1 tablespoon grated Parmesan cheese
1 teaspoon Vegeta

Prepare the pancake batter in the usual way using the listed ingredients. Also add melted butter to the mixture. Leave to rest for about 20 minutes, and then make eight thin pancakes.

Spread the filling over them preparing it in the following manner:

Mix the olive oil, basil leaves, crushed garlic, Parmesan cheese and pepper into a homogenous mixture.

Fold the pancakes twice to make quarters, fry them in hot butter on both sides. Pour cream over them, roasting juices (about 6 tablespoons), sprinkle with Vegeta and grated Parmesan cheese. Arrange the pancakes in an oven-proof casserole and place in a preheated oven to bake for 8 - 12 minutes.

If you plan to serve the pancakes as an independent meal, prepare them according to the listed ingredient quantity. At festive occasions you can serve them together with a combination of various pastas.

Preparation and cooking time: about 1 hour
(1 serving amounts to 444/1865 Cal/J)

In Slovakia potatoes are not served merely as pommes frites or pureed, but you find them in a tasty and ingenious soup or dumplings with meat stuffing. The head chef of the Bratislava restaurant named "Slovenskà reštauracija", František Janata, revealed to the Vegeta cooking team his recipe for traditional potato pancakes.

Potato Pancakes Young Homemaker Style (serves 4 - 6)

Ingredients:
1 kg/2 lbs potatoes
200 g/7 oz flour
100 ml/3 1/2 fl oz mineral water
200 ml / 7 fl oz milk
2 eggs
250 g/ 9 oz salami (ham-based)
2 cloves garlic
ground pepper, salt, parsley
frying oil
1 tablespoon Vegeta

Note: In the Slovakian cuisine it is traditional to fill these pancakes with various types of finely cut sautéed meat, but in such cases ham is not included.

Peel the potatoes, grind finely and drain. Add the flour, milk and salami cut into small strips. Add the mixed eggs, a little salt, pepper, chopped parsley, crushed garlic and Vegeta. Finally add the mineral water.

Heat a little oil in a saucepan and spread evenly the mixture formed as pancakes. Fry the pancakes on both sides until golden.

You can serve these potato pancakes - "placke" - with various salads or sour cabbage in wintertime.

Preparation and cooking time: about 45 minutes
(1 serving amounts to 577/2454 Cal/J)

For many non-Czechs, the first encounter with Czech cuisine is tasting festive dishes such as roast meat with Czech dumplings. But there are also many economical and simple dishes which may be served with the excellent Czech beer, such as the following potato dumplings, richly spiced up with garlic and other seasonings.

Bramboraky

(serves 4)

Ingredients:
1 kg / 2 pounds potatoes
200 ml / 7 fl oz milk
3 tablespoons flour
3 eggs
50 g/ 1 1/2 oz smoked bacon
3 - 4 cloves garlic
piment, marjoram
pepper, salt
frying oil
1 tablespoon Vegeta

Grate the peeled potatoes finely, pour over hot milk. Add the diced bacon, mixed eggs, flour, crushed garlic, ground piment, marjoram, pepper, a little salt and Vegeta.

Mix all the ingredients well and spoon the mixture into hot oil, press lightly so they are formed as small thick pancakes. Fry on both sides, because bramboraky should be crunchy. Arrange bramboraky on absorbent paper towels and serve hot or cold with beer.

If you serve salad or sour milk with bramboraky, you will have a small and tasty independent meal.

Preparation and cooking time: about 40 minutes
(1 serving amounts to 441/1883 Cal/J)

Note: You should prepare all the bramboraky ingredients ahead of time so that cooking time is as short as possible and the dish tastier.

Vegetables keep on respiring after having been harvested. Therefore, it is very important how to preserve their freshness. The best place for vegetables in an Electrolux refrigerator is in the vegetable drawer where the temperature and moisture are optimal to keep them fresh until used. In case products need to be frozen rapidly, the Electrolux freezer has a separate rapid freezing partition.

Note:
Rapid freezing helps to avoid damage of the product tissue structure, and this helps preserve the vegetable freshness

vegetable dishes

vegetable dishes

Although its Italian name means "great soup", minestrone is a complete Italian dish all cooked in one pot. The greater the variety of included products, especially vegetables, the better. From one season to another, from one region to another, minestrone will differ: in Toscana it is prepared with baby beans, peas, celery and courgettes; in Genoa with pumpkin and cabbage and as many as three types of pasta; in Milan it contains almost everything that can be found in a garden. Inspired by this famous Italian soup we created our Vegeta Minestrone.

Vegeta Spring Vegetable Minestrone

(serves 4-6)

Ingredients:

2 carrots
30 g / 1 oz celeriac
200 g / 7 oz green string beans
100 g / 4 oz peas
2 courgettes
3 tablespoons oil
50 g/2 oz dry-smoked bacon
1 onion
3 cloves garlic
1 beef-soup cube
wild thyme
basil leaves
marjoram
1 tablespoon tomato pureé
1-2 potatoes
80 g/3 oz small pasta
parsley leaves
grated Parmesan cheese for serving
1 tablespoon Vegeta

Fry the diced carrots, celeriac and onion briefly in the oil. Add the chopped green beans, peas and finally the courgette rounds. Mix the finely chopped bacon, garlic and Vegeta into the vegetables. Add the soup cube and pour in 1l/1 3/4 pints water. Simmer slowly, and add the seasoning: wild thyme, basil leaves and marjoram, tomato pureé,. diced potatoes and pasta. Cook until all the ingredients are tender and cooked.

Dilute with a little water if necessary and add the chopped parsley. Serve after mixing in the grated Parmesan cheese or serve the cheese separately.

Preparation and cooking time: about 1 hour
(1 serving amounts to 311/1307 Cal/J)

There is a Club-Restaurant by the Moscow MHAT, the theater of Chekow and Stanislavsky, worthy of their art. The head chef there, Alexander Tikhonow, makes traditional Russian dishes in a new, creative way. The Vegeta team was especially impressed by his version of the famous Russian borshch, and to learn that the characteristic red color depended on using the redder beetroots.

Home-Made Borshch with Vegeta

(serves 6-8)

Ingredients:
1 kg/2 lbs beef for soup
1 beef soup cube
1 small cabbage
500 g/1 lb carrots
500 g/1 lb potatoes
500 g/1 lb beetroot
150 g/5 oz onion
50 g/2 oz butter
50 ml/2 fl oz vinegar
sugar
1 tablespoon tomato purée
bay leaf, parsley, pepper
2 cloves garlic
200 ml/7 fl oz sour cream
1 tablespoon Vegeta

Place the meat into about 2 1/2 l / 4 pints of water. Add the Vegeta, soup cube and a pinch of salt. Leave to simmer slowly. Remove the foam from the surface occasionally. Cut the meat into small strips.

Peel the beetroot, grate it coarsely and place in a small amount of water to which you have added the vinegar. Cook for 20 - 30 minutes.

Dice the cabbage or cut it into strips, dice the potatoes and onion, and grate the carrots coarsely. Put the cabbage into the meat soup and cook for10 -15 minutes. Add the potatoes and continue cooking.

Fry the onion and the carrots in the previously heated butter, add the tomato purée and simmer. Mix in the cabbage and the beetroot. Season with pepper, bay leaf, sugar and finely chopped garlic. Finally add the meat pieces and cook briefly. If necessary dilute the borshch a little, and add a small amount of vinegar, if liked.

Pour the borshch into a soup bowl or serve it in small separate bowls. Sprinkle with parsley and swirl a tablespoon of sour cream into each separate portion.

Note: The characteristic red color of your borshch depends on the beetroot used, so choose the redder ones. You may decorate the soup with lemon slices, whipped cream and cranberries.

Preparation and cooking time: about 1 hour and 30 minutes
(1 serving amounts to 514/2160 Cal/J)

Various wheat "kashas" are highly esteemed in Poland, quite independently of the world healthy food trend. When we were told by Michael Logozzo, the well-known American chef working in Warsaw that the last supper on the Titanic started with the famous Polish barley soup, we decided that we had to try it in our Vegeta kitchen. It is not only famous, but also very good for you.

Krupnik

Barley and Vegetable Soup

(serves 6)

National

Note: Do not throw away the water you cooked the barley in, because barley water is a valuable dietary product, especially in treating stomach disorder.

Ingredients:
150 g/5 oz barley
20 g/ 3/4 oz dry mushrooms
100 g/3 1/2 oz onion
50 g/2 oz dry-cured bacon
150 g/5 oz carrots
2 celeriac stalks with leaves
500 g/1 lb potatoes
50 ml/2 fl oz oil
2 bay leaves
2-3 garlic cloves
salt, black pepper
parsley or dill
1 tablespoon Vegeta

Place the barley in water and leave it to soak, best overnight. Drain off the water and cook in 2l/ 2 1/2 pints of slightly salted water. Soak the dry mushrooms, drain after a short while, dry on paper towels and chop into small pieces.

Fry the chopped onion and diced bacon briefly in hot oil, add the prepared mushrooms. You can also add some thinly sliced fresh mushrooms. Mix with the diced carrots and potatoes, bay leaf, Vegeta and braise. Add the barley together with the liquid, celeriac, freshly ground pepper, finely chopped garlic and cook about ten minutes.

Dilute the soup with a little water, if necessary. Before serving take out the celeriac stalks and sprinkle with chopped parsley or dill.

Preparation and cooking time: about 1 hour
(1 serving amounts to 305/1281 Cal/J)

The name of this cold refreshing soup means "soaked bread", although it is based on a large quantity of vegetables. Besides, it is prepared in Malaga with veal bouillon, in Cordoba it is thickened with cream and flour, in Cadiz it is served hot in winter, and in Andalusia hard boiled eggs are added.

Preparation and cooking time: about forty minutes plus chilling time
(1 serving amounts to 196/827 Cal/J)

Gazpacho
- Spanish Chilled Vegetable Soup
(serves 6 - 8)

Ingredients:

800 g/1 1/2 lb tomatoes
2 green peppers
1 small cucumber
100 g/4 oz onion
100 g/4 oz one-day-old white bread
4 cloves garlic
100 ml/14 fl oz olive oil
2-4 tablespoons wine vinegar
salt, freshly ground pepper
800 ml/1 1/2 pints water
1 tablespoon Vegeta

Ingredients for garnishing:

1 green pepper
1 onion
1 large tomato
100 - 150 g/ 4 - 5 oz white bread

Add the Vegeta to 1 1/2 pints of water, cook and cool. Dice the bread and soak it in a small quantity of this soup. Dice the pepper, cucumber, onion and tomato. Put the vegetables in an electric blender, add the bread, garlic, olive oil, wine vinegar and the chilled Vegeta stock. Blend until smooth. (If the blender is too small for all of the ingredients, repeat the procedure several times with smaller portions).

Place the Gazpacho into a bowl, season with freshly ground pepper and add salt to taste. Leave covered in the refrigerator for about three hours to chill well.

Before serving finely chop the vegetables for garnishing: the tomato, onion and pepper. Dice the bread and fry in a small quantity of butter, if wished.

Place the diced bread and vegetables separately in small bowls and arrange them around the bowl of chilled Gazpacho.

Note:
The refreshing taste of this soup is achieved not only by chilling it, but also by choosing the vegetables carefully.

Provencal colors, sounds and aromas have inspired many artists, so creativity is also found in many a dish from this picturesque region. The Vegeta team was surprised by the many variants of the famous Salade Niçoise encountered from place to place, with new ingredients added to the basic ones along with the Provencal aromatic herbs.

Preparation and cooking time: about 20 minutes
(1 serving amounts to 505/2122 Cal/J)

Salade Niçoise

(serves 4)

Ingredients:

1 lettuce head
500 g / 1 lb tomatoes
200 g / 7 oz can tuna
100 g / 4 oz black olives
4 hard-boiled eggs

Salad dressing: (approx. 350 ml / 12 fl oz)
200 ml / 7 fl oz olive oil
50 ml - 100 ml / 3 - 4 fl oz wine vinegar
50 ml / 3 fl oz water
2 teaspoons dry Provencal herbs
(thyme, rosemary, marjoram, sweet basil, garden-sage)
salt
freshly ground pepper
1 tablespoon Vegeta

First prepare the salad dressing. Chop the Provencal herbs finely, mix with the wine vinegar, water and Vegeta. Add the olive oil, season with pepper, add salt to taste and mix well. Leave to rest for at least 1 hour. (The quantity of ingredients is sufficient for this dressing to be used several times).

Clean the lettuce, wash the leaves, drain and arrange on 4 plates. Quarter the tomatoes and hard-boiled eggs, drain the tuna and arrange the ingredients on the lettuce leaves together with the olives.

Sprinkle the salad with part of the dressing and place the remainder in the refrigerator to be used later, when required.

Salade Niçoise has become part of menus worldwide, and can be prepared by varying some of the ingredients. You can garnish the salad additionally with small slices of onion, diced fresh pepper, string beans, chopped celery stalks, radish, green olives, basil leaves, and if you want a really piquant version, replace the tuna with anchovies.

Note:
Even with all the changes this will still be the original Salade Niçoise. In southern France it is often served as a between-meals course, or as an independent dish, and it may also be found as baguette sandwich filling.

Preparation and cooking time: about 30 minutes
(1 serving amounts to 333/1398 Cal/J)

Lamb's Lettuce with Duck Breast

(serves 4)

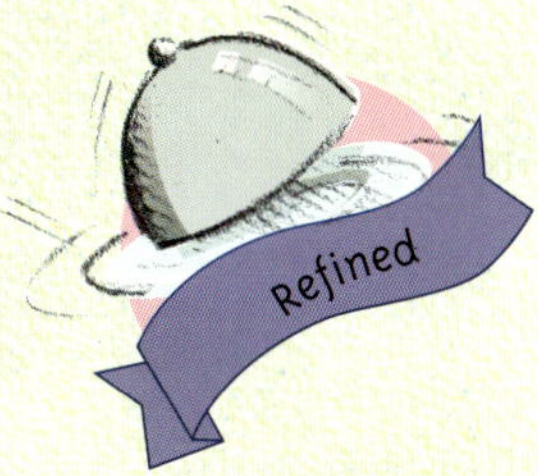

At Okrugljak, the well-known Zagreb restaurant at the foot of Sljeme slopes, both traditional and modern cuisine is served. The following recipe is a contribution and creation of the head chef, Srećko Lončar, and was created in honour of the 900th anniversary of the founding of the Croatian capital.

Ingredients:
2 duck breasts
100 ml/4 fl oz oil
40 g/ 1 1/2 oz butter
salt
white pepper
30 ml / 1/2 fl oz cognac
400 g/ 14 oz lamb's lettuce
cider vinegar
1 teaspoon Vegeta

Remove the duck's breast meat from the bone together with the skin so that you get 4 pieces. Carve the skin in a net-like pattern so that the meat becomes tender more easily when cooked.

Clean and wash the lamb's lettuce. First pour the oil into the frying pan, then add the butter. Season the duck's breasts with salt and pepper. Place the meat pieces skin down onto the heated oil/butter mixture in the frying pan. Brown well, turn the other side down and fry for about ten minutes more at low heat.

Place the breasts on a board, cut into slices and return to the hot oil/butter mixture in the pan, sprinkle with Vegeta.

Fry for a short while, sprinkle with cognac and put alight a fire to flambé.

Arrange the lamb's lettuce in the plate center, dress with a mixture of the oil, cider vinegar and salt.
Arrange the sliced duck, season with pepper and pour over the sauce left over after frying.

Note:
Do not fry the meat slices too long or they will become tough. Instead of lamb's lettuce you may use some other type of lettuce, depending on the season. In this case cut the salad leaves into wide strips.

Marinated Aubergines and Courgettes

(serves 4)

A specialty from the Toscana cuisine is a summer refreshment made with typical Mediterranean vegetables, prepared in a characteristic manner. Besides being unusual, simple to make and tasty, it is very practical because it will keep in the refrigerator for several days. It goes especially well with grilled meat.

Ingredients:

1 kg/2 lbs aubergines
1 kg/2 lbs courgettes
salt
100 ml/ 4 fl oz sunflower and olive oil mixture
4 cloves garlic
200 ml / 7 fl oz wine vinegar
2 red chilli peppers
fresh basil leaves
1 tablespoon Vegeta

Peel the courgettes and aubergines and cut into 1/2 cm / 1/4 inch slices. Season them with salt, the aubergines first in order to extract the bitter juice, and then dry well with paper towels.

Cut the garlic finely, and the peppers into small rings.

Arrange the aubergines and courgettes in an oil covered baking pan, sprinkle with a small quantity of oil and place into the oven to bake for about ten minutes.

Arrange the cooked aubergines and courgettes in a dish sprinkling each row with garlic slices. Cook the wine vinegar, Vegeta, chilli peppers and 150 ml / 1/4 pint of water mixture briefly and pour over the vegetables while still hot. Sprinkle with fresh basil leaves and leave covered overnight.

You may serve the marinated aubergines and courgettes as a separate meal or as a side dish to different meals.

Note: You may keep the marinated vegetables refrigerated for several days. If you serve them with slices or cubes of white sheep cheese or a slice or two of prosciutto, you will have a really picturesque and tasty Mediterranean meal.

Preparation and cooking time: about 45 minutes plus marinating time
(1 serving amounts to 254/1066 Cal/J)

Preparation and cooking time: about 45 minutes plus cooling time
(1 serving amounts to 297/1248 Cal/J)

Asparagus with Green Sauce (serves 4)

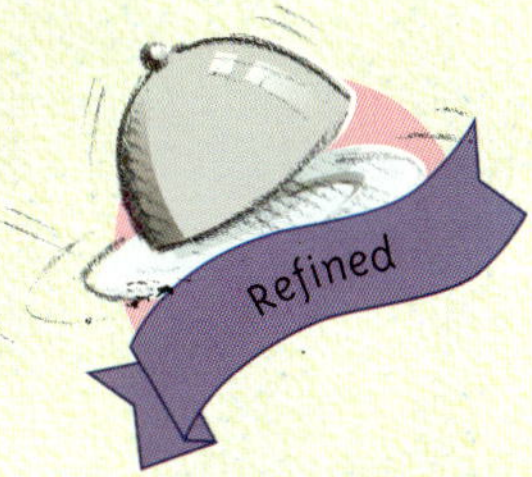

Originally, asparagus grew wild, but ever since it started to be cultivated, gourmets enjoy it not only in spring, but all the year round.

Many consider it to be tastiest simply boiled and served with sauce. Instead of the famous Sauce Hollandaise, try them with the equally well-known green sauce.

Ingredients:
1 kg / 2 lbs asparagus

Sauce:
4-5 hard-boiled eggs
100 ml / 4 fl oz wine vinegar
100 ml / 4 fl oz water
1 teaspoon sugar
1 tablespoon estragon mustard
100 ml / 4 fl oz oil
freshly ground pepper
1 bunch of parsley
1 bunch of dill
2 bunches of fresh chives
100 ml / 4 fl oz sour cream
1 tablespoon Vegeta

Clean the asparagus and trim any hard ends, tie into a bunch, and stand it upright in a tall saucepan filled with boiling salted water. The water should reach half way up the height of the asparagus bunch so that it cooks in water while the asparagus tops should cook in the steam above the water. Cook the asparagus carefully for 10 - 15 minutes until the lower parts become tender. Remove them from the water, drain and cool.

Prepare the sauce in the following manner: add sugar and Vegeta to the vinegar and wine vinegar mixture, cook briefly and leave to cool.

In the meantime chop the hard-boiled eggs, parsley, dill and chives finely.

Add the mustard, oil, chopped hard-boiled eggs, parsley, dill and chives to the cooled down wine vinegar and Vegeta mixture. Then add the sour cream, season with pepper, mix well and salt to taste.

Place the prepared sauce in a cool place for 1- 2 hours.

Arrange the cooked asparagus on plates, pour over the sauce and garnish with ham and hard-boiled egg slices, if wished.

Note:
Apart from with asparagus, you can serve the green sauce in combination with other dishes such as boiled vegetables, boiled meat, fish or as various fresh salad dressing.

Gratinated (Oven-baked) Asparagus

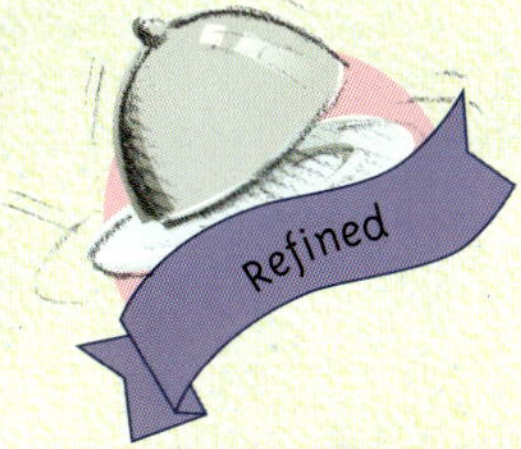

(serves 4-8)

As far back as 3000 years ago the Chinese considered asparagus to have healing qualities. Today it is considered as a means of purifying the body, and in Germany there are asparagus festivals. Cream of asparagus soup, asparagus with tomatoes and mozzarela or covered with fried bread crumbs, eggs or gratinated are only some of the (excellent) ways to prepare it.

Ingredients:

1 kg / 2 lbs asparagus
80 g/ 3 oz butter
1 teaspoon sugar
8 - 10 slices of cooked ham
150 g/ 5 oz Gauda cheese
2 tablespoons grated Parmesan cheese
1 tablespoon Vegeta

Scrape the lower two thirds of the asparagus, wash and arrange so that the tops are at the same level, tie in a bunch and cut off the hard tips.

Pour water into a tall narrow saucepan for cooking aparagus, add the sugar, salt, 20 g/ 3/4 oz butter and Vegeta. When the water comes to the boil put the asparagus into the saucepan so it stands upright. Cook for 15-30 minutes (depending on the type of asparagus, green asparagus is more tender and needs to be cooked for a shorter period of time than the white).

If you do not have a special saucepan for cooking asparagus, use a wider saucepan.

Drain the cooked asparagus, remove the thread, and wrap 3-4 pieces of asparagus in a slice of ham. Arrange them in an oven-proof dish, add a couple of tablespoons of the cooking water. Sprinkle with grated cheese and grated Parmesan cheese. Arrange butter slices on top and bake for about 15 minutes in a preheated oven at 220 °C/ 425 °F/ gas 7.

Note:
You can make a tasty soup using the leftover asparagus cooking water.

Preparation and cooking time: about 45 minutes
(1 serving amounts to 374/1564 Cal/J)

Artichokes with Peas

(serves 4)

Many know it only as a type of dry flower brought back from summer holidays as a souvenir, but artichokes are a favorite among the people where it grows, in Dalmatia. Thus we have prepared it Dalmatian style using green peas instead of broad-beans. Artichokes are very healthy, sometimes they grow wild and today they are grown in fields, for example in the area near Trogir. If you can not buy fresh artichokes, use canned ones.

Ingredients:

- 8 artichokes
- lemon juice
- 4 tablespoons bread crumbs
- 100 ml / 4 fl oz olive oil
- 4 cloves garlic
- parsley
- salt
- pepper
- 500 g/1 lb peas
- 1 tablespoon Vegeta

Clean the artichokes, removing the tough leaves, cut off the hard stalks and the sharp leaf tops.

Briefly boil the artichokes in salted water to which you have added lemon juice and then drain.

Prepare the stuffing in the following manner: Add the chopped parsley and garlic, pepper and Vegeta, and mix well. Spread the artichoke leaves and spoon the mixture between the leaves. Put the peas in a saucepan and arrange the artichokes on top, heads up. Pour oil over them, season with a little salt and pour cold water over them so they are covered almost to the top. Cook over a low heat for about one hour, depending on the type of artichoke. When most of the liquid evaporates, add a little more oil, if wished.

Arrange the artichokes on a heated platter together with the pea sauce, garnish as desired and serve.

Preparation and cooking time:
about 1 hour and 30 minutes
(1 serving amounts to 298/1254 Cal/J)

Note:
The artichokes may be prepared with young broad-beans instead of peas.

In Turkish cuisine, seasonings are used in a superb way and if one chances upon the wide variety of products found in the Misir or Egyptian markets, one of the many in Istanbul, as was the case with the Vegeta team, new combinations are made. That is the case in this imaginative oriental dish, seasoned by parsley leaves, garlic, sweet red pepper powder, pepper, dill, saffron, thyme, various mixtures... You can taste all these flavours in just one dish made with Vegeta created by the Podravka Culinary Center.

Stuffed Courgettes

(serves 4)

Ingredients:

4 large courgettes
4 tablespoons oil
250 g/9 oz meat (beef or lamb)
1 onion, 2 - 3 tomatoes
bunch of dill
50 g/ 2 oz rice
salt, pepper, parsley
1 teaspoon mint
2 cloves garlic
several drops of Tabasco Sauce
1 tablespoon Vegeta Sauce

Slice the courgettes in half lengthwise and remove the pulp with a teaspoon and sprinkle with a little salt.

Then prepare the stuffing:

Fry the meat in 2 tablespoons of oil, but only briefly, until it changes color. Add the grated onion, chopped tomatoes, fry briefly again and remove from the heat. Mix in the rice previously dipped in hot water and drained.

Add chopped parsley, dill, mint, crushed garlic cloves, pepper, a few drops of Tabasco Sauce, part of the courgette pulp and Vegeta. Add 2-3 tablespoons of water to this mixture and salt to taste. Fill the courgette shells with this filling, arrange them in an ovenproof baking dish and place a slice of tomato on each. Pour over a mixture made of 200 ml/ 8 fl oz salted water and two tablespoons of oil. Bake covered in the oven for about 30 -40 minutes at a temperature of about 200 ° C/400 ° F/gas 6.

Note: In the Turkish fashion, you can serve yogurt with garlic to gowith this very tasty and light dish, making it additionally refreshing. Or you can add a garnish to taste.

Preparation and cooking time: about 1 hour
(1 serving amounts to 417/1750 Cal/J)

Summer Vegetable Pot

(serves 4)

The popularity of Chinese cooking and preparing food in a wok reminds us, especially during summer, of the possibility of a tasty, unusual and very attractive meal out of a small quantity of meat, various vegetables and other ingredients, like the following:

Ingredients:

- 300 g/ 10 oz round of pork
- 100 g/ 4 oz carrots
- 2 peppers
- 4 spring onions
- 1 teaspoon tomato purée
- 1 tablespoon concentrated mushroom soup
- 2 cloves garlic
- 1 chilli pepper
- 4 tablespoons oil
- parsley
- 1 tablespoon Vegeta

Cut the pork into thin strips, do the same with the carrots, peppers and spring onions. First place the meat in the preheated oil, and fry it quickly on all sides, stirring continuously. Add the carrots, fry briefly (add a little water, if necessary).

Then add the peppers, onion, crushed garlic, chopped chilli pepper and Vegeta. Sauté, adding water gradually. When almost cooked add the tomatoes and a spoonful of the mushroom soup concentrate mixed with water and cook briefly. Sprinkle with chopped garlic and serve.

You can serve this dish as an independent meal or garnished with rice, potatoes, or broad pasta.

Note: In order to make this dish tastier, it is important to fry the meat in well preheated oil and to cook it well and quickly on all sides.

Preparation and cooking time: about 25 minutes
(1 serving amounts to 374/1573 Cal/J)

Preparation and cooking time: about 1 hour and plus at least one hour for resting the pastry
(1 serving amounts to 658/2766 Cal/J)

Leek Quiche

(serves 4)

Even mega-stars like Sharon Stone, Tina Turner, Elton John or Steven Spielberg were fascinated by the "cuisine of the sun", prepared by one of the leading French chefs, Roger Verge at his restaurant "Le Moulin de Mougins" (situated in an old olive-pressing plant).

The Vegeta cuisine team was particularly impressed by his vegetable specialties.

Ingredients:

Pastry:

250 g/ 9 oz flour
120 g/ 4 oz butter
1 egg, salt
1 tablespoon sour cream

Filling:

500 g/ 1 lb leeks
200 ml / 7 fl oz cream
2 eggs
chives
salt, pepper
1 teaspoon Vegeta

Add the slices of butter to the flour and rub them in with your finger-tips and then with your palms. Add the mixed egg, cream and a pinch of salt. Knead into dough. Form a ball and leave in the refrigerator to rest for one hour.

Clean the leeks, wash well, cut lengthwise and boil briefly in boiling salted water. Drain the leeks, cut into slices or cubes leaving some cut into sticks for decorating the quiche. Roll out the chilled pastry thinly and place in a buttered baking pan or oven-proof dish 18-20 cm / 7-8 inches in diameter. Carefully line with pastry the edges of the pan or dish, too. Prick the pastry with a fork and leave to rest for about 30 minutes. Then arrange the leeks over the pastry. Mix the eggs, cream, a teaspoon of chopped chives, pepper and Vegeta and pour over the leeks.

Decorate the top with leek sticks and put into a preheated oven to bake for 35-40 minutes at 200 °C / 400 °F / gas.

Note:
Instead of leeks you can use vegetables of the season, or depending on the occasion, i.e. broccoli, cauliflower, spinach, carrots or the like.

78

Sataraš (Satarash)

(serves 4)

The ingredients for a classical summer salad can be transformed in a split second into a new combination, a very tasty, simple-to-prepare and almost forgotten dish.

It can be served with grilled meat or fish, or you may deep-freeze it and use it for garnishing (cooked beans, sautéed meat...), and if you stir an egg into it, you will be surprised by the new taste.

Ingredients:

- 500 g/ 1 lb peppers
- 500 g/ 1 lb tomatoes
- 1 large onion
- 5 tablespoons oil
- 1 teaspoon sugar
- salt, pepper
- 1 tablespoon Vegeta

Clean the peppers and cut into small pieces. Slice the onion thinly. Peel the tomatoes, remove the seeds and cut into pieces.

Fry the onion to a golden color in preheated oil in a wide saucepan, add the sugar, and then the prepared peppers. When the pepper begins to turn tender stir in the tomatoes and Vegeta, continue braising until the liquid evaporates. Season the sataraš with salt and pepper to taste. You may add some Soya sauce, if desired. Sataraš can be served in various ways: as hot hors d'oeuvres, or a small dish with different garnishing.

Note: A wide saucepan is needed for cooking sataraš. This helps the liquid to evaporate as quickly as possible, and the peppers to remain firm and to produce the desired aroma.

Preparation and cooking time: about 20 minutes
(1 serving amounts to 227/954 Cal/J)

Simple and inexpensive

Due to its availability, low price and nutritional value cabbage appears on the menu in various guises. It is best consumed fresh or pickled as salad. When it is cooked, the time it is exposed to heat should be short so that the valuable vitamins are not destroyed. The following dish can be a vegetarian meal, but it can also be garnishing for sautéed meat.

Cabbage Vegeta Style

(serves 4)

Ingredients:

1,5 kg/3 lbs cabbage
3 tablespoons oil
50 g/ 2 oz dry-cured bacon
1 onion
salt
pepper
caraway seed
100 ml / 4 fl oz white wine
20 g/ 3/4 oz butter
parsley leaves
1 tablespoon Vegeta

Quarter the cabbage, and then cut into wide strips. Fry the diced bacon and onion in preheated oil. Add the cabbage. Season with salt, add the caraway seeds, Vegeta and mix well. Braise the cabbage briefly, pour over a little water and wine, cover and braise over a low heat for about 25 minutes, stirring occasionally. Remove from the heat, add the butter, pepper and chopped parsley.

Serve this cabbage with boiled bacon or mashed potatoes.

Preparation and cooking time: about 35 minutes
(1 serving amounts to 355/1492 Cal/J)

Note: Add the wine at the very beginning and do not exceed the cooking time, so that the cabbage becomes tender, but still remains firm. It will be tastier too.

The Good Soldier Shveyk succeeded, of course, in charming the Vegeta cuisine team. From Prague and his guest house "U Kalicha", which is reminiscent of the time described in Yaroslav Hashek's novel, the team returned with lots of tasty impressions and the following dish, typical for Bohemia.

Red Cabbage Bohemian Style

(serves 4)

Ingredients:
1 kg/2 lbs red cabbage
4 tablespoons oil
1 onion
caraway seeds
1 teaspoon flour
30 g/ 1 oz sugar
2-3 tablespoons wine vinegar
1 tablespoon Vegeta

Shred the cabbage into strips, boil briefly in a little water and drain. Fry the chopped onion in oil, add the sugar, cabbage, caraway seeds and Vegeta. Dust with flour, mix and leave to braise. When almost done add the vinegar and salt to taste.

Preparation and cooking time: about 35 minutes
(1 serving amounts to 232/974 Cal/J)

Note:
You can serve braised potatoes or mashed potatoes with this dish, or as excellent garnishing for roast duck or some other poultry.

Gourmets will not pass over this traditional old-time rural specialty consisting of pickled turnips and gnocchi, especially if it is served with a piece of dry-cured boiled meat or ribs. You can cook the meat separately, and pour the cooking water over the turnips so that they are tastier. Beans can be cooked together with the turnips, and then you will have an economical independent meal, all in one pot. The turnips can be cooked in a larger quantity, refrigerated, and added to other dishes.

Pickled Turnips with Gnocchi

(serves 4)

Ingredients:

1 kg/2 lbs pickled turnips
40 g /1 1/2 oz dry-cured bacon
4 cloves garlic
1 tablespoon flour
bay leaf
salt, peppercorns
1 tablespoon Vegeta

Garnishing:

potato gnocchi

Rinse the turnips in water and drain if too sour. Boil in water to which you have added the bay leaf, peppercorns and Vegeta. Blend the bacon and garlic together in a blender or chop finely, add to the turnips and continue cooking until the turnips are tender. When almost done, add the flour which you have mixed with a little water. Salt to taste.

While the turnips are cooking prepare the potato dough gnocchi, or cook some deep-frozen ones just before serving.

Serve the turnips and gnocchi sprinkled with bread crumbs fried in butter.

Note:
If you prepare turnips this way, the sauce should neither be too watery nor too thick. So be careful how much water you cook them in.

Preparation and cooking time: about 1 hour
(1 serving amounts to 226/952 Cal/J)

Glass-ceramic cooking plates
They are fully controlled and switch off when your roast is done, according to your wishes. When the desired temperature has been reached in the center of the roast, the oven switches off automatically and a buzzer lets you know the meat is done. The good looks and easy-care features of the glass-ceramic cooking plates and their great efficiency in comparison with traditional hot-plated are increasing their popularity. What sets Electrolux glass-ceramic hot-plates apart is High Light Technology which allows precise plate temperature regulation, and greater heating speed when required.

dishes with mushrooms and eggs

1. *Champignons/Button Mushrooms Spread*
2. *Champignons/Button Mushrooms with Eggs*
3. *Champignons/Button Mushrooms Roulade*
4. *Fine Mushroom Stew*
5. *"Ozalj" Noodles with Mushrooms*
6. *Eggs à la Flamenco*
7. *Eggs à la King*

dishes with mushrooms and eggs

This simple, but unusual dish with a new taste is a good idea for a vegetarian meal.

Champignons/Button Mushrooms Spread (serves 4)

Ingredients:
250 g/ 9 oz champignons/button mushrooms
100 g/ 3 1/2 oz onion
2 cloves garlic
40 g/ 1 1/2 oz butter or margarine
1 tablespoon tomato ketchup
1 tablespoon sour cream
40 g/ 1 1/2 oz mayonnaise
salt, pepper
1 teaspoon Vegeta

Wash the champignons/button mushrooms, clean and chop finely or roughly blend in a blender. Fry the chopped onion to a golden colour in preheated oil, add finely chopped garlic, champignons/button mushrooms and Vegeta. Braise until all the liquid evaporates, and then cool. Add ketchup to the prepared mushrooms, sour cream, mayonnaise and chopped parsley. Season with pepper, stir well and add salt, if necessary. Chill the spread in the refrigerator. Serve with black bread, cucumbers, onion, radishes or tomatoes, or hard-boiled eggs.

Cooking time: about 45 minutes plus preparation time
(1 serving amounts to: 195/822 CalJ)

The ingredients used for this dish allow its preparation the year round. Excellent and tasty it can be served as hors d'oeuvres or a complete supper. For instance, you can use the same mixture as a spread on pieces of bread, sprinkle with grated cheese and bake in the oven briefly.

Champignons with Eggs

(serves 4)

Ingredients:
500 g/ 1 lb champignons/button mushrooms
4 tablespoons oil
4 hard-boiled eggs
150 g/5 oz mayonnaise
80 g/ 2 1/2 oz Gauda cheese or similar
salt, pepper
Tabasco Sauce or hot pepper
1 tablespoon Vegeta

Wash and clean the champignons, dry them and slice thinly. Heat the oil in a large saucepan, add the champignons and braise until the water evaporates. When almost done add salt, pepper, several drops of Tabasco Sauce and the Vegeta. Stir well, cook briefly and cool. Add the finely chopped eggs and the mayonnaise. Mix lightly and place in an ovenproof casserole, arranging cheese slices over the top. Bake briefly in a preheated oven (about 10 minutes).

You may serve various fresh or pickled salads with this tasty dish.

Preparation and cooking time: about 30 minutes
(1 serving amounts to: 581/2443 Cal J)

Note: Dry the champignons/button mushrooms well before slicing them. Braise them in preheated oil in a broad pan so that they remain juicy.

This following recipe was brought by the Vegeta cooking team from the Tyrol, but it is also often found in the international cuisine. It was found both very tasty, and practical because it can be prepared in advance and baked just before serving.

Ingredients:
5 tablespoons flour
400 ml/ 14 fl oz milk
5 eggs, salt

Filling:
350 g/12 oz champignons
15 g/ 1/2 oz dry mushrooms
30 g/ 1 oz butter
1-2 tablespoons bread-crumbs
2 eggs, 1-2 cloves garlic
1 teaspoon estragon mustard
100 ml/ 4 fl oz sour cream
pepper, parsley
1 tablespoon Vegeta

Champignon/Button Mushroom Roulade

(serves 4-6)

Mix well the flour and about 100 ml/4 fl oz cold milk. Bring to the boil the remaining milk which you have seasoned with salt, remove from the heat, stir in the prepared flour mixture and continue cooking until the mixture becomes thick, stirring continuously. Mix the egg yolks into the chilled mixture one by one, and finally fold in the egg whites beaten to peaks.

Line a baking tin about 30x40 cm/12 - 16 inch in size with baking paper, oil the paper evenly and spread the prepared mixture over it. Bake for about 10-15 minutes at a temperature of 200 °C/400 °F.

Take out the baked roulade placing it on a moistened cloth and roll it up.

Prepare the filling in the following manner:

Fry the thinly sliced champignons/button mushrooms in butter. Add the soaked, drained and chopped dry mushrooms and Vegeta. Braise briefly, and leave to cool. Afterwards add the mustard, pepper, chopped parsley,

sour cream, bread crumbs and mixed eggs.

Spread the filling over the unfolded roulade, roll it up again, place it in an oiled baking tin or oven-proof casserole. Cover with aluminum foil and bake in the oven about 20 minutes. Cut the roulade into slices and serve with boiled vegetables, for instance carrots, broccoli, cauliflower, peas.

Preparation and cooking time:
about 1 hour twenty minutes
(1 serving amounts to: 319/1342 Cal J)

Exploring interesting places in Slovenia, the Vegeta cooking team found itself on the Ježovnik family estate "Jelenov Greben". Besides the herds of deer, and wild game specialties, we were especially interested in the mushroom growing farm, and several excellent mushroom specialties which inspired us to create this mushroom stew.

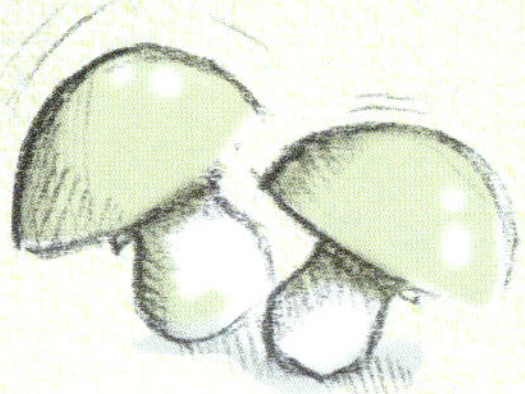

Fine Mushroom Stew

(serves 4)

Ingredients:
600 g/1 1/4 lb mushrooms (champignons/button mushrooms,
beech-mushrooms, yellow chanterelles,
mushrooms)
10 g/1 1/2 oz dry mushrooms
3 tablespoons oil
40 g/1 1/2 oz smoked bacon
1 onion
2 carrots, celeriac leaves
pepper, salt
bay leaf, marjoram
thyme
3 cloves garlic, parsley
100 ml / 4 fl oz sour cream
1 teaspoon cornstarch (Gussnel)
wine vinegar
200 g/7 oz potatoes

Clean the mushrooms and cut into largish pieces. Dice the bacon finely, slice the carrots thinly, and chop the onions.

Fry the bacon and onion in preheated oil, then add the carrots and continue frying.

Add the prepared, drained and chopped dry mushrooms and the fresh ones. Fry well, sprinkle with Vegeta and braise adding hot water, when necessary.

When the mushrooms are half-cooked, add the bay leaf, celeriac leaves, marjoram, salt to taste and continue cooking slowly. When the stew is almost done, pepper to taste.

Stir in the mixture which you have prepared combining cornstarch flour diluted with water, sour cream, chopped garlic and parsley. Add some vinegar. While you are making this stew, cook some peeled potatoes separately. When the potatoes are done mash them coarsely and mix into the stew. Serve with separately prepared mashed potatoes. Or you can cook a large quantity of diced potatoes and mix them into the stew, diluting with a little water, if necessary.

Preparation and cooking time: about 45 minutes
(1 serving amounts to: 337/1418 Cal J)

Note:
Instead of vinegar you can add a little white wine.

"Ozalj" Noodles with Mushrooms

(serves 4)

Each mushroom harvest is an inspiration for mushroom pickers to invent a new dish depending on the mushroom nature has produced. The surroundings of the town of Ozalj are rich in mushrooms and it was from that area that the Vegeta team learned of this recipe. A very savory dish made here with cultivated mushrooms.

Ingredients:

300 g/11 oz broad noodles
1 small onion
3 tablespoons oil
origano
2 cloves garlic
400 g/ 14 oz fresh mushrooms
(various types)
salt, pepper
100 ml / 4 fl oz white wine
30 g /1 oz butter
150 g/ 5 oz fresh cottage cheese
200 ml / 8 fl oz cream
1 egg yolk
parsley leaves
1 tablespoon Vegeta

Clean the mushrooms and slice them thinly. Chop finely the onion, garlic and parsley.

Fry the onion and mushrooms in preheated oil, add the origano and Vegeta.

Pour over the wine and braise until the mushrooms are tender. Add the garlic and season with pepper.

Cook the mushrooms in salted water. Be careful that they do not overcook. Drain them.

Place the butter, noodles, fresh cottage cheese, cream mixed with the egg yolk and the prepared mushrooms in a broad pan. Heat and sprinkle with parsley.

Note:
If you combine several kinds of mushrooms the dish will be even tastier.

Preparation and cooking time: about 30-35 minutes
(1 serving amounts to: 598/2514 CalJ)

94

Andalusia is famous for its many and highly diverse cultures, the wild rhythm of the corrida, the fire of flamenco and the passionate poetry of Garcia Lorca.

This Spanish region shows through in the following dish prepared with specific ingredients which together result in an exceptional taste.

It can be prepared in Spain in almost any season, and the choice of ingredients can be adapted to what is in season, and to personal tastes.

It has very interesting variants if asparagus tips are added. Smoked bacon as well as typical home-made sausages are some of the possible ingredients for this Spanish dish.

Eggs à la Flamenco

(serves 4 - 6)

Ingredients:

1 aubergine
1 - 2 red peppers
1 onion
100 g/3 1/2 oz hulled peas
100 g/3 1/2 oz green beans
400 g/14 oz tomatoes - pelati
1 tablespoon tomato puree
50 ml/1 1/2 fl oz olive oil
4-5 cloves garlic
20 g/ 3/4 oz flour
salt, Tabasco sauce
4-6 eggs
60 g/2 oz smoked bacon
1 tablespoon Vegeta

Dice the aubergine, salt and leave for a short time to rest. Rinse with water and drain. In the meantime chop the onion finely, and cut the peppers into small pieces. Cook the peas and green beans in boiling hot water until half-done, and drain.

Heat the oil in a broad saucepan, and fry the pepper and onion. Add the drained and diced aubergine previously dredged in flour, the crushed garlic and fry briefly. Then add the tomatoes - pelati together with the juice, the tomato purée, several drops of Tabasco Sauce, the peas, green beans and Vegeta and braise for about 10 minutes. Place the prepared vegetables in an ovenproof plate, make wells for the eggs and place an egg into each. Arrange bacon slices around the eggs and bake for about 15 minutes at 220 °C/400 °F/gas 6.

Note: The number of eggs will depend on whether the dish will be served as hors d'oeuvres or the main dish.

Preparation and cooking time: about 45 minutes plus marinating time
(1 serving amounts to: 254/1066 Cal J)

Eggs à la King

(serves 4)

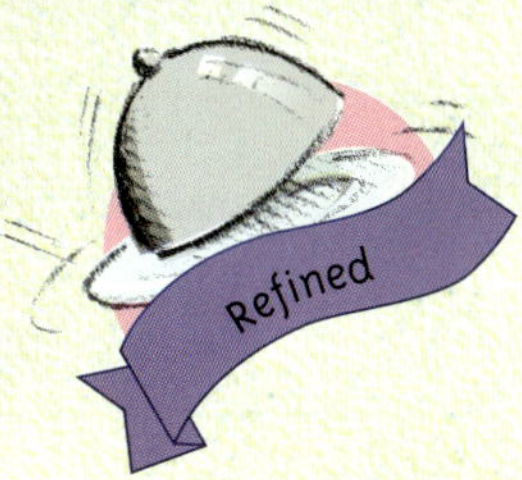

The egg, symbol of perfection and the source of life, once was a very rare, expensive food. Now it is available the year round. It is highly esteemed for its valuable ingredients and the different possibilities it offers in preparing various dishes. The Iberian peninsular or, in other words, Spain, has especially imaginative ways with eggs, and that is where the following recipe comes from.

Ingredients:

8 eggs
90 g/ 3 oz butter
30 g/ 1 oz flour
500 ml / 16 fl oz milk
100 ml / 4 fl oz cream
lemon juice
salt, pepper
150 g/ 5 oz rice
parsley
20 g/ 3/4 oz grated Parmesan
1 tablespoon Vegeta

Hard boil the eggs (about 5 minutes), and carefully clean them of their shells. Prepare the bechamel sauce: heat 50 g / 1 1/2 oz butter, mix in the flour and fry very briefly. Pour in the cold milk, add the Vegeta and cook for about 5 minutes until the sauce thickens, stirring continuously. Add a little lemon juice, pepper and cream.

Fry the washed and drained rice briefly in a separate saucepan in the remaining butter. Pour in about 300 ml / 1/2 pint water, season with a little salt and leave to cook until half-done. Mix in the chopped parsley and arrange the rice in an oven-proof casserole. Halve the eggs lengthwise and arrange them over the rice, pour over the prepared sauce and sprinkle with grated cheese. Place to bake about 15 minutes in a preheated oven at 220 ° C/425 ° F/gas 7.

Note:
If you wish to serve this dish as a more wholesome meal, add some ham slices, cheese or some other ingredient.

Preparation and cooking time: about 30 minutes
(1 serving amounts to: 602/2529 Cal J)

Electrolux
INTELLIGENT SOLUTIONS FROM SWEDEN

Thanks to the baking probe with which the Electrolux oven is equipped, the roasting process is fully controlled, and will be stopped the moment your roast has reached the optimal temperature depending on the type of meat and manner of cooking you have selected.

Note:
For those who like the real taste of meat, roasting at high temperatures is recommended.

meat dishes

1. Chicken Liver Parfait
2. Stuffed Boiled Chicken
3. Julia's Chicken Stew
4. Adobo
5. Chicken Primošten Style
6. Chicken Obara
7. Turkey Legs Styrian Style
8. Chicken Breast in Orange Sauce
9. Turkey Dijonnaise
10. Stuffed Turkey Escalopes
11. Marinated Chicken Parisienne
12. Chicken Kiev
13. Chicken with Sesame
14. Stuffed Chicken
15. Pork Fillet with lemon
16. Suki-yaki
17. Pork Stew à la Czarda
18. Boiled Beef à la Salzburg
19. Pork Tenderloin with Sour Cream
20. Stuffed Veal Breast
21. Meat Roll "à la Peka"
22. Stuffed Roast in Wine
23. Boiled Veal Knuckle
24. Pork Knuckle on the Spit
25. Roast Ribs with Peppers
26. Oven Goulash
27. Ismir Escalopes
28. Multi-Coloured Barbecue
29. Pork Knuckle New Style
30. Wild Game Ragout
31. Wild Game Goulash
32. Rabbit in a Pot

meat dishes

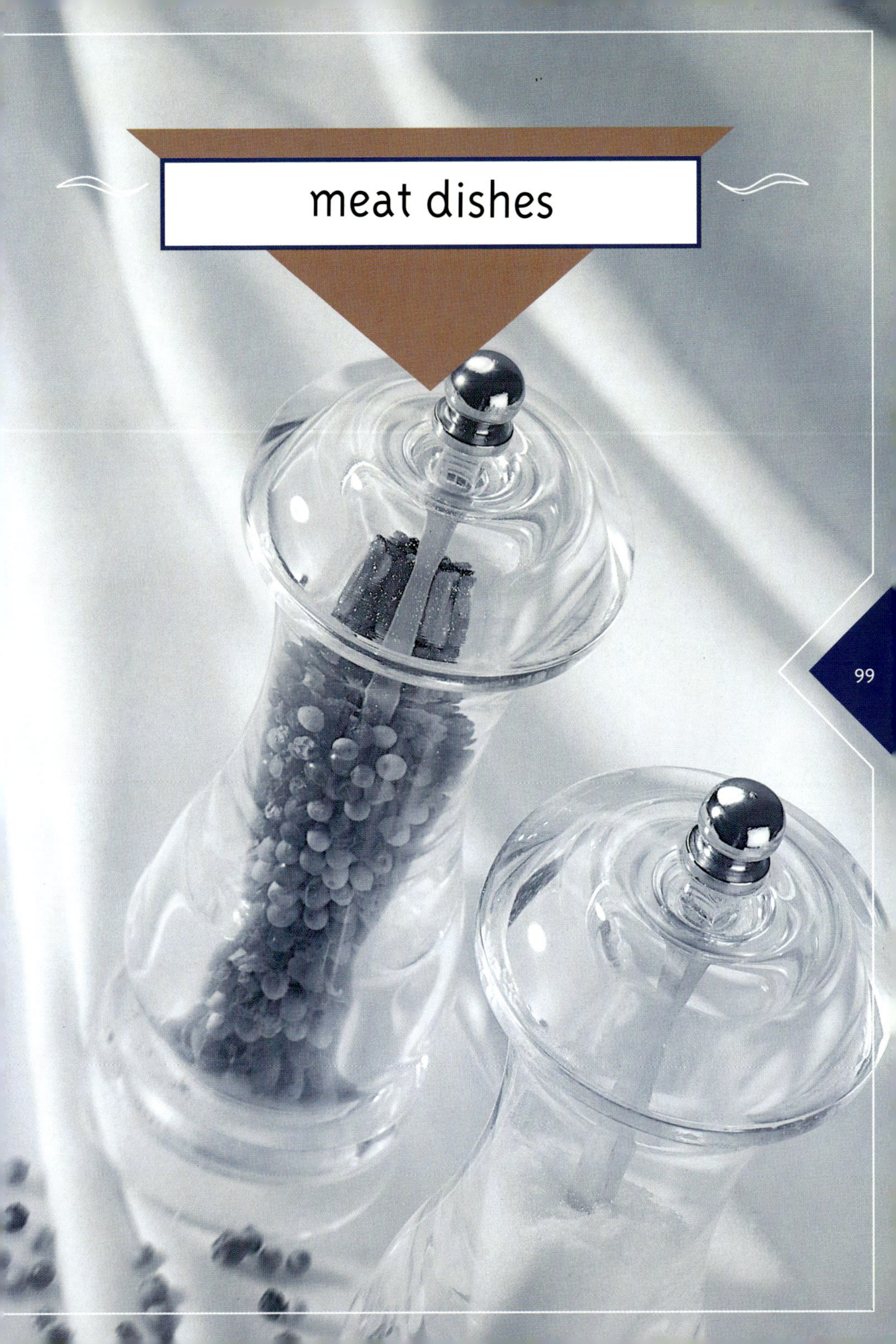

The following hors d'oeuvres dish is one of the choicest in French cuisine, which, according to many gourmets, still leads the world. The perfection of the ingredient combination surprises with its refined taste. The dish is also known under the name mousse.

Note: If you prepare the aspic with Vegeta it will shorten cooking time and make preparation more simple in comparison to the traditional method.

Chicken Liver Parfait

(serves 6)

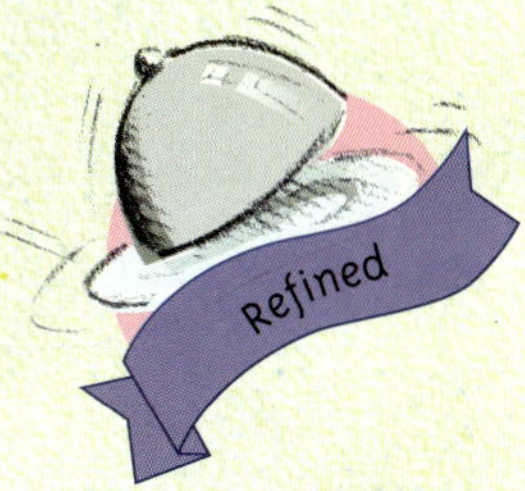

Ingredients:

500 g/1 lb chicken liver
40 g/ 1 1/2 oz smoked bacon
1 onion (35 g/ 1 oz)
60 g/ 2 oz root vegetables (carrots, celeriac, parsley)
salt, pepper
80 g/ 1 1/2 oz butter
100 ml / 4 fl oz cream
9 sheets gelatin
1 tablespoon cognac
1 tablespoon rum
50 ml / 2 fl oz white wine
1 tablespoon Vegeta

Preparation and cooking time:
about 1 hour plus preparation time
(One serving amounts to 325/372 Cal J)

Preparation of the aspic with the addition of Vegeta: cover the gelatin with cold water and soak. Boil for about five minutes 500 ml / 16 fl oz of water to which you have added one tablespoon of Vegeta and a little white wine. Add the drained gelatin and let it dissolve. Afterwards heat this soup with gelatin once again until it comes to the boil, strain and cool. Cut the bacon into small slices, the root vegetables into rings, the onion into slices and fry in 30 g/ 1 oz butter. Add the liver, fry and then braise. Add a little water when necessary. Season the braised liver with salt, and season with pepper when completely done. Press the chilled liver and vegetable mixture through a sieve (or blend in a blender until it attains a creamy consistency).

Mix the remaining butter until creamy, add the liver, cream, 100 ml / 4 fl oz of the prepared gelatin, cognac, rum, white wine and mix until fluffy. Season to taste. Fill one dish or several small ones with the mixture and place in the refrigerator to chill overnight. Heat the remaining aspic a little, pour into a tin and leave to chill.

When serving shake the parfait out onto plates. Decorate with diced aspic and serve with toasted bread.

In the Istrian hinterland, on Sovin polje not far from Buzet, in the old reconstructed oil plant, Nevio Sirotić is developing village tourism with the help of his family. "Toklarija" is a place which offers domestic and traditional dishes, and thanks to Nevio's mother Judita, Vegeta's cooking team tasted a light, economical, tasty dish cooked in one pot, that used to be prepared for the weddings in past times.

Stuffed Boiled Chicken

(serves 6)

Ingredients:

1 hen (about 1 1/2 kg / 3 lbs)
150 g/ 5 oz carrots
80 g/ 2 1/2 oz celeriac

Stuffing:

50 g/ 1 1/2 oz sheep cheese
120 g/ 4 oz bread
1 egg
freshly ground pepper, salt
parsley
2 cloves garlic
1 tablespoon Vegeta

Clean the hen and vegetables. Dice the one-day-old bread. Grate the cheese coarsley, chop the garlic and parsley.

Mix the prepared bread with mixed egg, cheese, parsley and garlic. Season with ground pepper and with salt. Stir well and stuff the chicken with this mixture. Sew up the opening or close it with the help of toothpicks.

Place the chicken in salted water together with the carrots and celeriac, a little salt and Vegeta. Cook slowly until the meat becomes tender. Take the chicken out of the soup, take out the stuffing and cut it into slices. Arrange together with cut pieces of meat on a preheated plate.

Decorate with boiled vegetables, pour part of the hot soup to which you may add some lemon juice over the food and sprinkle with chopped parsley. If you wish you may also serve grated horseradish.

Note:
It is important to place the stuffed chicken to cook in boiling water for this will help the stuffing keep its firmness and shape.

Preparation and cooking time: about 1 hour and 30 minutes
(One serving amounts to 876/3679 Cal J)

Julia Frank, reporter and first lady of Hungarian gastronomy, rekindled the Vegeta cooking team's interest in the famous Hungarian cuisine. Her 42 cooking books (12 translated into other languages in 1992) have been printed in 4 million copies and earned her a place in the Guiness Book of World Records. With much reason if one judges on the basis of the following typical Hungarian dish, to which Julia has added her own personal culinary touch.

Preparation and cooking time: about 40 minutes
(One serving amounts to 803/3373 Cal J)

Julia's Chicken Stew

(serves 4 - 6)

Ingredients:

1 chicken (about 1 1/2 kg/3 pounds)
50 g/ 1 1/2 oz smoked bacon
1 onion
2-3 green peppers
2 tomatoes
100 ml / 4 fl oz sour cream
150 g/ 5 oz champignons/ button mushrooms
1 tablespoon red powdered pepper (some of it hot)
1 tablespoon flour
3 cloves garlic
pepper, salt,
1 tablespoon oil
1 tablespoon Vegeta

Clean the chicken, wash, cut into small pieces and season with salt. Cut the bacon into thin slices, chop the onion and garlic. Cut the washed and cleaned champignons/button mushrooms into thin slices, the pepper into rings, and the tomatoes (previously peeled) into cubes. Briefly fry the bacon and onion in a small quantity of oil, remove from the heat, add the powdered red pepper and mix a little. Add the chicken, fry on all sides, then add the champignons/button mushrooms, peppers, garlic, pepper and Vegeta. Braise covered (in its own juices without adding water) about 15 minutes over low heat. Stir the stew accasionally.

When the meat becomes tender add the tomatoes. Mix the flour and sour cream with about 100 ml / 4 fl oz water, mix into the stew and cook briefly. Serve broad noodles with this dish adding cucumber salad as desired.

Adobo

(serves 4)

Far-Eastern cuisines are in at the moment. Although it belongs to this group geographically, the cuisine of the Philippines is quite different, if ingredients are compared.

The Spanish influence has made it similar to European cooking in some ways, but the specific seasonings and ingredients take it far away from Europe. This is quite evident in respect to the most typical Philippine dish coming from the Mindanao district. We were introduced to it by Dr Hololina Sero Gomez, who was specializing in Zagreb.

Ingredients:

600 g/ 1 1/4 lb chicken (1/2 chicken)
2 cloves garlic
pepper
3 tablespoons Soya sauce
2 tablespoons wine vinegar
1 tablespoon Vegeta

Prepare the Soya sauce, wine vinegar, pinch of pepper, crushed garlic and Vegeta Mixture in a bowl.

Cut the chicken into pieces and place in a small pot. Pour over the prepared mixture, stir and add about 100 ml/3 1/2 oz of water. Cover the pot and cook slowly until the meat becomes tender. Part of the liquid must evaporate so that the sauce has the necessary consistency and absorbs all the aromas.

If you wish, you can take pieces of the prepared chicken out of the sauce and fry shortly in another saucepan in a small quantity of oil. Pour over the remaining Soya sauce. You can serve Adobo with various kinds of braised vegetables or the original Philippine dish "Vegetable guisado".

Preparation and cooking time: about 40 minutes
(One serving amounts to 498/2083 Cal J)

Note: This tasty dish will keep 2-3 days outside the refrigerator and as long as a week if placed in the refrigerator.

Although there are only small quantities of prosciutto, Prosecco (Sherry) and capers in the following dish which can be, thanks to refrigerators, prepared in any season, they give the recognizable Dalmatian taste. The dish will be equally tasteful if you substitute the chicken with lamb.

Chicken Primošten Style

(serves 6)

Ingredients:

1 chicken (about 1 1/5 kg / 2 1/2 lbs)
1 tablespoon oil
30 g/ 1 oz flour
150 g/ 5 oz onion
60 g/ 2 oz prosciutto or smoked bacon
6 canned peeled tomatoes (pelati) "Podravka"
60 ml / 2 fl oz Prosecco
2 tablespoons capers
500 g/ 1 lb peas
500 g/ 1 lb new potatoes
salt, pepper
3 cloves garlic
parsley leaves
1 tablespoon Vegeta

Cut the chicken into pieces, season with salt and dust with flour. Fry in hot oil until brown on all sides. Take the chicken pieces out of the pan, add the chopped onion, the diced bacon or prosciutto and fry briefly in the remaining oil. Add the chopped tomatoes, braise briefly and pour over the Prosecco (Sherry). Mix in the capers, peas and place the chicken back with the ingredients into the pan. Sprinkle with Vegeta and pour over a little water. Braise slowly until the meat becomes tender. Add water when necessary. Before the meat becomes tender add the peeled, half-cooked new potatoes. Season with pepper, stir in the chopped garlic and parsley.

Note:
This dish may be prepared without adding potatoes. In this case serve it with potato gnocchi.

Preparation and cooking time: about 45 minutes
(One serving amounts to: 966/4062 CalJ)

Traditional

Chicken Obara

(serves 4 - 6)

Obara is a Slovenian cuisine specialty. This soup-like dish is often served as the main course. It is prepared with various meat, in some parts even frog legs, while the best known obara is the one prepared with chicken and served with buckwheat žganci (hard boiled buckwheat mush). In the past obaras were thickened with fried flour, whereas today the meat and vegetables are fried, dusted with flour, and water or soup is poured over them, with the addition of the characteristic marjoram, wine vinegar or wine.

Ingredients:

600 g/ 1 1/4 lb chicken
40 g/ 1 1/2 oz oil
1 carrot
1 parsley root
30 g/ 1 oz celeriac
1 tablespoon flour
salt, pepper
lemon rind
marjoram, bay leaf
a little wine vinegar
1 tablespoon Vegeta

Fry chicken pieces on all sides in hot oil. Add the chopped onion, carrot, parsley and celeriac cut across or into sticks and fry briefly. Season with salt, dust with flour, stir well and pour over 8-10 ml / 3-4 fl oz water. Add the Vegeta, pepper, marjoram, bay leaf and lemon rind. Cook slowly until the meat becomes tender. When cooked, season the obara with vinegar.

Serve with boiled potatoes.

Note:
In the more original version the obara is served with buckwheat žganci.

Preparation and cooking time: about 45 minutes
(One serving amounts to: 367/1543 Cal J)

Turkey meat is inexpensive now and may be bought cut in various pieces. Thanks to this, many new, simple and easily available dishes have been created like the following one made with turkey legs. We recommend it especially for autumn and winter days.

Note: This dish may be prepared with chicken legs. In this case the cooking time will be significantly shorter.

Turkey Legs Styrian Style

(serves 4)

Ingredients:
2 turkey legs (about 80g / 2 1/2 oz)
salt, freshly ground pepper
nutmeg
100 g/ 3 1/2 oz carrot
100 g/ 3 1/2 oz parsley - root
100 g/ 3 1/2 oz celeriac root
parsley
1 large onion
6 tablespoons oil
2 bay leaves
wild thyme
1/4 l/ 8 fl oz white wine
2-3 tablespoons wine vinegar
4 tablespoons freshly grated horseradish
1 tablespoon Vegeta

Cut the onion into slices. Cut the carrots, parsley and celeriac root into sticks. Chop the parsley leaves. Remove the skin from the turkey legs, rub salt, freshly ground pepper and nutmeg into the meat. Heat the oil and fry the turkey legs on all sides slowly so that they change color. Arrange the cut carrots, parsley and celeriac root in an oven-proof casserole, place the turkey legs on top together with the oil. Sprinkle with wild thyme, parsley and Vegeta. Pour over the wine and vinegar, cover the casserole with a lid or aluminium foil. Roast for about one hour in the oven preheated to 180° C/350° F/ gas 4. Add some more wine and water during the cooking when necessary. When the meat becomes tender, take the casserole out of the oven, remove the meat from the bones and cut it into slices. Arrange on a preheated platter together with the vegetables and roasting juices, and sprinkle with grated horseradish. Serve with boiled potatoes and chopped parsley.

Preparation and cooking time:
about 1 hour 20 minutes
(One serving amounts to: 767/3221 Cal J)

Chicken Breasts in Orange Sauce

(serves 4)

Dennis Valčić is a Croatian who has been living in Canberra for more than 30 years now. Although he manages a fast food restaurant, he has written the "Croatian Cookbook" in his new homeland, and also has presented his Australian cuisine in his old homeland. The recipes are interesting and unusual, because the settlers from Europe, Asia and other continents all brought their culture with them. This dish is a tasty example.

Ingredients:

8 small chicken breast fillets
150 ml / 5 fl oz orange juice
grated rind of one orange
1 orange
20 g/ 3/4 oz brown sugar
1 teaspoon spicy mustard
2 tablespoons oil
2 teaspoons cornstarch (Gussnel)
1 tablespoon Vegeta

Heat the oil and half the butter in a large saucepan, slowly fry the chicken on all sides for about 8 minutes. Remove the chicken and place on a preheated plate.

Place the remaining butter into the pan, the grated orange rind, orange juice and sugar, and cook for 3-4 minutes, stirring continuously.

Add the cornflour mixed with a little water, and finally the peeled orange cut into thin rounds. Cook briefly, dilute the sauce with water if necessary and season with salt to taste. Arrange the chicken fillets on a preheated plate, place an orange round on each, pour over the hot sauce.

Serve with boiled rice, and various boiled vegetables as desired.

Preparation and cooking time: about 35 minutes
(One serving amounts to: 4[illegible]7/1796 CalJ)

Note:
Be careful not to overcook chicken fillets or they will become too dry.

Turkey Dijonnaise

(serves 6)

The turkey originally comes from America, and besides being popular in many other countries, it is the traditional holiday food in America at Christmas and on Thanksgiving Day. Vegeta's guest, Michael Logozzo a Newyorker of Italian descent, surprised us with his unusual, modern, American/Italian style of cooking turkey. Excellent.

Ingredients:

1 1/3 kg/ 2 1/2 lbs turkey breast
1 tablespoon Dijon Mustard
1 tablespoon mustarda (mustard
containing roughly ground mustard-seed)
freshly ground black pepper, salt
100 ml / 3 fl oz dry white wine, or
50 ml / 2 fl oz vermouth
30 g/ 1 oz butter
300 ml /1/2 pint cream
2-3 apples, 2-3 pears
50 ml / 2 fl oz oil
1 tablespoon Vegeta

Marinate the turkey: spread a mustard and Vegeta mixture over the meat. Leave to rest about 2 hours at room temperature.

Pour the oil into the roasting pan, place the marinated turkey breast into it, season with a small quantity of pepper, and roast for about 90 minutes at 180° C/ 250° F/ gas 4. Pour water over the roast occasionally and baste with wine or vermouth when almost done.

Heat the butter in a saucepan, add the apples and pears which you have peeled and cut into slices. Braise briefly, add the cream, the mustard you have gathered from the roast surface and the roasting juices. Lower the heat and cook the sauce slowly for about 5-10 minutes. Season with more pepper and salt to taste and pour over the meat you have cut into slices. Serve hot with boiled broad macaroni, rice or corn soufflé.

Preparation and cooking time: about 1 hour plus 30 minutes marinating time
(One serving amounts to: 839/3511 Cal J)

Preparation and cooking time: about 40 minutes
(One serving amounts to: 700/2941 Cal J)

Stuffed Turkey Scallops

(serves 4)

Although many Croatians would not substitute Turkey Zagorje style with "mlinci" for any other turkey recipe, if one wishes to eat something lighter and healthier, non-fat white poultry meat comes to mind, especially turkey breast meat.

Ingredients:

8 turkey breast scallops
(about 60 g/ 2 oz)
4 tablespoons oil
lemon juice
salt, pepper
200 g/ 7 oz spinach
20 g/ 3/4 oz butter
1/2 small onion
1-2 cloves garlic
100 g/ 3 1/2 oz cheese
Trappist or Gauda
30 g/ 1 oz flour
50 ml / 3 fl oz white wine
1 tablespoon Vegeta

Beat the scallops lightly with a wooden kitchen pounder, sprinkle with Vegeta and lemon juice.

Briefly boil the cleaned spinach, drain and chop. Fry the chopped onion to a golden colour in hot melted butter, add the spinach, chopped garlic, pepper, salt, mix all the ingredients and cool.

Place the prepared spinach mixture on each scallop with a slice of cheese on top. Fold the scallops, pound the edges a little or fix together with toothpicks. Flour the scallops a little and fry in hot oil. Fry on each side for about 7 minutes. Finally add a little water, the wine and simmer briefly.

Arrange the scallops on a heated plate and pour over the hot sauce. Serve boiled rice with this very tasty, filling, yet light meal.

Note:
You can serve this dish with boiled vegetables.

Spices are a separate chapter in cooking because they add to the aroma, taste and appearance of food, improving our appetite and also help the food be digested better. Thanks to them this marinade has completely changed some very ordinary dishes. Especially their taste.

Marinated Chicken Parisienne

(serves 4)

Ingredients:
1 chicken
Marinade:
lemon juice (about 4 tablespoons)
2 tablespoons oil
salt, pepper
2 cloves garlic
parsley
rosemary
bay leaf
1 tablespoon Vegeta

2 eggs
1 tablespoon flour
frying oil

Marinade: Mix the lemon juice, oil, a little salt, pepper, crushed garlic, finely chopped parsley, several crushed rosemary leaves, and one small bay leaf.

Cut the chicken into pieces, place in a porcelain bowl and pour over the marinade. Stir all the ingredients, leave to rest about two hours in the refrigerator. The meat should be turned over occasionally so as to marinate equally on all sides. Drain the surplus marinade if necessary and season the chicken a little bit more with salt. Dip each piece of meat in a mixture of eggs and flour and fry in hot oil.

Serve with lemon slices and lettuce salad.

Preparation and cooking time:
about 40 minutes plus marinating time
(One serving amounts to: 650/2732 Cal J)

The following recipe is an example of how ordinary everyday chicken stuffed with only a little herb butter can become interesting, tasty and new. And besides - it's an internationally accepted dish.

Chicken Kiev

(serves 4)

Ingredients:
2 pcs chicken breasts
100 g/ 3 1/2 oz butter
2 tablespoons chopped parsley and chives, salt, pepper
lemon juice
flour, eggs, breadcrumbs for coating
frying oil
1 tablespoon Vegeta

Note: You can use the butter mixture as an addition to various scallop dishes.

Mix the butter until fluffy, add the chopped parsley and chives, season with pepper and Vegeta. Mix well and form this butter mixture into a thin roll. Wrap in foil and place in the refrigerator to chill and become firm. Lightly pound the chicken breasts (4 scallops), season with a little salt and sprinkle with lemon juice drops.

Cut the chilled butter into four pieces. Place a piece on each of the four scallops, roll up. Coat the rolls with flour, mixed eggs and breadcrumbs, and fry in hot oil for about ten minutes.

Serve with rice-and-peas or fried potatoes.

Preparation and cooking time: about 1 hour
(One serving amounts to: 332/1397 Cal J)

Very nutritious and valuable seeds are becoming more widely used in the modern cuisine, especially sesame seeds. They have been known by the Chinese cuisine for as long as several thousand years, but they have been used in sweets and savory dishes in other countries as well. We added sesame seeds to the classical mixture for coating chicken, which you may serve hot or cold as finger-food.

Chicken with Sesame

(serves 4-6)

Ingredients:

800 g/ 2 lbs chicken breast fillet
lemon juice
about 2 tablespoons Soya sauce
salt, pepper
flour, 2-3 eggs for coating
300 g/10 oz sesame seeds
2 tablespoons breadcrumbs
frying oil
1 tablespoon Vegeta

Cut the chicken into large strips. Sprinkle with lemon drops and Soya sauce and sprinkle with Vegeta. Leave to rest. Cover with flour, dip into mixed eggs which you have seasoned with a little salt and pepper and finally roll them in a sesame and bread crumb mixture.

Deep-fry in hot oil at medium temperature until golden. Take out and place on absorbent tissue.

You can serve the chicken with sesame hot or cold with various sauces, for instance tartare.

Preparation and cooking time: about 40 minutes
(One serving amounts to: 293/1227 Cal J)

Stuffed chicken is a favorite whether it is the rural or town Croatian cuisine and was not omitted in the representative monograph cookbook "Croatia at Table", the authors of which are also part of the Vegeta gastronomic team. This time the stuffing is not made with liver but is both more simple, more refined and refreshing.

Stuffed Chicken

(serves 6)

Ingredients:

- chicken (about 1 1/2kg/
- lbs)
- ;o ml/2 fl oz oil
- uice of half a lemon
- 20 g/ 4 oz bread or rolls
- oo ml / 4 fl oz milk
- 3o g/ 2 1/2 oz butter
- eggs
- epper
- utmeg
- unch of parsley
- tablespoons Vegeta

Spread the chicken inside with a lemon juice and Vegeta mixture. Season with salt to taste. Prepare the stuffing. Dice the bread or rolls finely and pour over the milk. Add egg yolks to the softened butter, then the pepper, grated nutmeg, chopped parsley and a teaspoon of Vegeta, mix well. Then add the soaked bread (if it is too wet, drain it), and egg whites beaten to peaks. Fold in gently. Raise the chicken skin beginning at the neck to prepare a place for the stuffing. Use a teaspoon to spoon the stuffing between the skin and the flesh. Put the remaining stuffing into the chicken opening. Close the opening and tie the legs to the chicken with thread. Place the chicken in a baking tin, pour over hot oil and a little water. Roast for about one hour to one hour and a half at 200° C / 400° F /gas 6. Baste the chicken during roasting with its own juices. You can serve this dish garnished with boiled peas, carrots and various fresh vegetable salads.

Preparation and cooking time
about 1 hour and 40 minutes
(One serving amounts to: 1171/4919 Cal J)

Note:
You can prepare the stuffing in many different ways, for instance with chicken liver or smoked bacon.

Pork Fillet with Lemon

(serves 4)

Just as the "Umjetnički paviljon" (Art Pavillion) in Zagreb attracts attention with its large exhibitions, the "Paviljon" restaurant in the same building attracts attention with its retrospective menu. One of the dishes, Pork Fillet with Lemon, was presented to restaurant guests and in the Vegeta TV show "Small secrets of Great Masters of Cooking" by its creator, the chef Stanko Erceg.

Ingredients:

600 g/ (1 1/2 lb) pork fillet
50 ml / 2 fl oz oil,
one lemon
salt, white pepper
10 g/ 1/2 oz flour
100 ml / 4 fl oz white wine
150 ml / 5 fl oz fresh cream
20 g/ 2/3 oz butter
parsley
1 tablespoon Vegeta

Cut the meat into 12 small slices. Beat them with a kitchen pounder, rub in a little Vegeta and salt. Sprinkle with part of the lemon juice. Leave to rest for a short while. Sprinkle with flour and fry in hot oil, firstly with the floured side down. When the meat turns golden-brown on both sides, pour wine over it and leave to stew slowly. When cooking is almost completed add the fresh cream, a little lemon juice, season with pepper, and add a little bit more Vegeta. Cook all the ingredients and add the butter when almost cooked. If you want more sauce, dilute it with a little water and thicken with cornstarch flour - Gussnel, if you wish.

Arrange the meat slices on a preheated plate, pour over the sauce, and garnish with peeled diced lemon rolled in chopped parsley.

Serve this simple and quickly prepared dish with "ducats" or potato croquettes.

Note: You can prepare veal fillet in the same way.

Preparation and cooking time: about 25 minutes
(One serving amounts to: 670/2814 Cal J)

Masumi Štiglić, who comes from Japan and is married to a Croatian, has publically demonstrated the art of flower arrangement, and came to the Vegeta kitchen to present the cuisine of the Land of the Rising Sun, an art in itself. The traditional Sukiyaki will be a pleasant and tasty surprise for your guests.

Preparation and cooking time: about 45 minutes
(One serving amounts to: 992/4149 Cal J)

Sukiyaki

(serves 4-6)

Traditional

Ingredients:

250 g/ 9 oz turkey fillet
250 g/ 9 oz beef fillet
250 g/ 9 oz pork cutlets (boned)
1 big onion
4 bunches spring onions
1/2 kg spinach
4 teaspoons sugar
3 tablespoons oil
200 ml / 7 fl oz Soya sauce, salt
150 g/ 5 oz rice noodles
300 g/ 10 oz rice
4-6 eggs
1 tablespoon Vegeta

Slice the meat, half-defrosted, into paper-thin slices and arrange on a plate to resemble a flower.

Place the cleaned and washed spinach on another plate, as well as peeled onion halves cut into thick slices and the spring onions cut diagonally.

Pour boiling water over the rice noodles and leave to rest for a short time until they become supple. Drain and place on a plate together with the vegetables.

Boil the washed rice in unsalted water (one to one ratio and do not drain or rinse).

Place the meat slices one by one into a special frying pan with thick bottom, fry each slice briefly until you have used all the meat. Mix and sprinkle with 4 teaspoons sugar. Stew briefly stirring continuously and pour over 100 ml/4 fl oz Soya sauce. Move the meat a little to the side and gradually add the vegetables until you have used up the whole quantity. Sprinkle with Vegeta, stew and pour over the remaining Soya sauce. The whole procedure of cooking this dish should not take longer than 8-10 minutes.

Note:
According to Japanese tradition rice is served in one bowl, and a fresh egg in another. The raw egg is mixed with chopsticks. Sukiyaki is prepared on a hot plate placed on the eating table. When the sukiyaki is cooked, hot pieces of food are taken from the central pan, each person dips it in the raw egg mixture in his bowl and eats the meat and vegetables with rice served in the other bowl in front of him.

Pork Stew à la Czarda

(serves 4)

Similar to goulash, but more refined, meat stew is probably one of the best known Hungarian dishes which has found its place in the international cuisine. It can be prepared from various types of meat, and the especially important ingredient are peppers, used here fresh and pickled, powdered, whole, cut into pieces and ground.

Ingredients:

600 g/ 1 1/4 lb pork leg
4 tablespoons oil
100 g/ 3 1/2 oz onion
10 g/ 1/2 oz ground red pepper
salt
100 g/ 3 1/2 oz tomato
2 peppers (green and red)
1 hot chilli pepper
1 tablespoon Vegeta

Cut the meat into sticks, slice the onion thinly, cut the cleaned peppers into small pieces, and dice the peeled tomato.

Fry the chopped onion in hot oil until golden. Lower the heat, add ground pepper and stir immediately. Add the meat, fry it on all sides, add the chilli pepper and sprinkle with Vegeta.

Pour over a little water and stew with the lid on. Stir the ingredients occasionally and add water when necessary, always in small quantities.

When the meat becomes half-tender, add the tomatoes and peppers, and you can add a teaspoon of flour mixed with a little water at the end, if you wish. Cook all the ingredients once again shortly.

As a side dish you can serve original Hungarian haluški or broad noodles.

Cooking time: about 30 minutes
(One serving amounts to: 527/2299 Cal J)

Note: In wintertime you can add preserved pickled peppers instead of the fresh ones.

Although the town of Salzburg is best known as the birthplace of Mozart and the place where Mozart Kugel sweets originate from, the Vegeta cooking team tasted many other excellent specialties in the typical Salzburg restaurants - the famous Salzburg floating islands, pretzels, ale soup, dumplings, duck... Especially impressive is the simple boiled beef dish garnished with vegetables. This traditional, healthy and tasty dish is prepared in other countries in a similar way as in Austria, often as we do, using Vegeta.

Cooking time: about 2 hours
(One serving amounts to: 534/2242 Cal J)

Boiled Beef à la Salzburg

(serves 4)

Ingredients:

1 kg/ 2 pounds beef
salt, peppercorns
1 - 2 carrots
1 parsley root
30 g/ 1 oz celeriac root
1 small leek
1 onion
2 cloves garlic
1 bay leaf
chives, nutmeg
1 tablespoon Vegeta

Cook the beef in salted boiling water. (The best piece of meat for preparing this dish is *tafelspic* - top of leg). When the water comes to the boil again, remove the foam from the surface and lower the temperature so that the meat simmers slowly.

In the meantime clean the carrots, parsley, celeriac, leek, onion and cut into bigish pieces. Add the vegetables and the garlic to the soup together with the bay leaf, pepper and Vegeta. Season with a little salt and continue cooking at a very low heat for about 1 1/2 to 2 hours.

When the meat becomes tender remove it, drain the soup and season with nutmeg. Cut the cooked meat into slices, arrange them on a hot plate, pour a little soup over them and sprinkle with chopped chives. The following garnishes go well with boiled beef: boiled vegetables (carrots, Brussels sprouts, leeks), potatoes with onions and horseradish sauce.

Note: To make the horseradish sauce which is a must when serving this specialty, use prepared soup: pour the hot soup over the diced rolls, add grated horseradish, season to taste and mix well.

Pork Tenderloin with Sour Cream

(serves 6-8)

Prague as a Central European classic, Muchine's Secession style and the literature in which Karl Chapek and Kafka blossomed, all come home to you with this dish which is a specialty of the famous Prague guesthouse named after the Good Soldier Shveyk.

Ingredients:

1kg/ 2 lbs pork tenderloin or fillet
40 g/ 1 1/2 oz smoked bacon
5 tablespoons oil
70 g/2 1/2 oz celeriac root
80 g/ 2 1/2 oz carrots
50 g/ 1 1/2 oz parsley root
60 g/ 2 oz onion
salt, peppercorns
allspice, bay leaf, thyme
2-3 tablespoons vinegar, lemon
20 g/ 3/4 oz butter
1-2 teaspoons sugar
1 tablespoon flour
200 ml / 7 fl oz sour cream
1 tablespoon Vegeta

Lard the meat with match-like sticks of bacon, season with salt and fry on all sides in hot oil. Add the vegetables and the onion cut into slices. Fry briefly all the ingredients. Add the allspice, bay leaf, thyme, ground pepper, two lemon slices and Vegeta. Stew covered adding water occasionally. Turn the meat and add the vinegar. When the meat becomes tender remove it and keep warm. Pureé the vegetables.

Let the sugar slowly turn into caramel in hot butter, add the pureéd vegetables, the flour diluted with a little water and cook all the ingredients briefly. Dilute the sauce with water, if necessary and stir in the sour cream.

Cut the meat into thin slices, arrange them on a plate and pour the hot sauce over them. Serve with Czech leavened dough dumplings, bread dumplings or croquettes.

Decorate with lemon slices, fresh cream beaten into peaks and cranberries.

Cooking time: about 1 hour and 15 minutes
(One serving amounts to: 476/1850 Cal J)

Stuffed Veal Breast

(serves 6)

The Boden Lake is shared by Germany, Switzerland and Austria. So are some traditional dishes such as stuffed veal breast. These are dishes which have their anthological place in Vegeta's cuisine.

Ingredients:

2 kgs (4 lbs) veal breast

Stuffing:

3 pretzels
250 ml/8 fl oz milk
1 onion, 2 bunches parsley
200 g/7 oz beech-stick mushrooms
50 g/ 1 1/2 oz butter
grated lemon rind
2 tablespoons lemon juice
1 tablespoon bread crumbs
2 eggs, salt, freshly ground pepper, nutmeg
50 ml / 2 fl oz oil
thyme
50 - 100 ml / 2 - 3 1/2 fl oz white wine
1 tablespoon Vegeta

Bone the veal breast, remove the excess fat, and cut an opening for the stuffing. (You can order the meat prepared in the above way from your butcher).

Prepare the stuffing: Slice the pretzels and pour over boiling milk. Leave covered to rest awhile. Chop the onion and parsley, cut the mushroom caps into thin strips, and dice the stands. Fry the onion, chopped parsley and mushrooms in 2 tablespoons butter. Fry for about 5 minutes until the liquid evaporates.

Mix the remaining butter until fluffy, add the lemon rind and juice, the soaked pretzels, mixed eggs, the prepared mushrooms and bread crumbs. Season with salt, pepper, add the nutmeg and Vegeta.

Stuff the veal breast and close the opening. Season the meat with a little salt on the outside. Heat the oil in the roasting tin and fry the meat well on both sides over a high heat. Add a little water into the tin and place in the oven to roast covered with aluminum foil for about one and a

137

half hours at 220° C/ 425° F (Gas Mark 7). When almost done, remove the aluminum foil and pour the wine mixed with a little thyme over the meat. Leave the veal breast for 15 minutes and then cut into slices, arrange on a plate and pour over the roasting juices. You can serve various types of fresh salad or boiled vegetables with the veal, or fried beech mushrooms, per taste.

Cooking time: about 2 hours
(One serving amounts to: 916/3829 Cal J)

Meat Roll "à la Peka"

(serves 8)

Živko Miočić, chef at the Feniks Konoba restaurant at Viškovo (in the hills above the town of Rijeka) prepares the excellent peka, čripnja, on an old-time traditional fireplace, with various kinds of meat. Nowadays, most people do not have a chance to cook in this manner which dates as far back as 3000 years ago, so the Vegeta cooking team has adapted the recipe to be an equally tasty specialty prepared in an up-to-date kitchen.

Ingredients:

2 kg/4 lbs veal, lamb or pork
4 tablespoons oil
60 g/2 oz smoked bacon (pancetta)
2 cloves garlic
parsley
pepper
salt
2 kgs/4 lbs potato
1 tablespoon Vegeta

Form the meat into a big scallop. Beat with pounder, season with a little salt and pepper.

Spread the prepared mixture over the meat and roll up. Fix with thread and season additionally with salt.

Pour the oil into the baking tin which replaces the peka, place in it the potatoes cut into thick slices. Season with salt, pepper and stir. Place the prepared meat roll on the potatoes and cover with aluminium foil and fix it to the sides of the tin so that the meat does not dry up during roasting. Place to roast in oven preheated to 220 °C/425 °F (Gas 7). When the roll is half done turn it over, and pour over a little water if necessary. Cook until done, about one and a half hours in all.

Remove the thread from the roast roll, cut into slices and serve with potatoes and salad to taste.

Cooking time: about 1 hour and 40 minutes
(One serving amounts to: 800/3360 Cal J)

The tastes of meat, fruit, spices and wine are a noble combination in this unusual roast. In autumn you may substitute the wine for stum (unfermented wine), and this tasty, unusual and sustaining dish will be even more aromatic.

Cooking time: about 30 minutes
(One serving amounts to: 661/2779 Cal J)

Note: You can prepare everything several hours before actual cooking time begins.

Stuffed Roast in Wine

(serves 6)

Ingredients:

750 g/ 1 lb 10 oz pork loin in one piece, boned

Stuffing:

2 pears
50 g/ 1 1/2 oz dried plums, pitted
lemon juice
120 g/ 4 oz one-day-old bread buns
2 tablespoons milk
50 g/ 1 1/2 oz butter
1 egg and one egg yolk
parsley
salt
pepper
4 tablespoons oil
50 g/ 1 1/2 oz smoked bacon
1 onion
1 bunch of soup vegetables (carrots, parsley, celeriac)
200 ml / 7 fl oz white wine
peppercorns
bay leaf
vinegar
1 tablespoon Vegeta

Prepare the stuffing first: dice the pears and plums (soak them in water first, if needed) and sprinkle with lemon juice. Dice the buns as well and sprinkle with 2 tablespoons milk.

Mix the butter (30 g/1 oz) with egg yolk and egg until fluffy, add the diced bread and fruit. Season with salt, pepper, add chopped parsley and mix all the ingredients well.

Prepare the meat: make a lengthwise cut and open up like a book so that you get a biggish scallop. Beat well with pounder, season with pepper and sprinkle with Vegeta. Spread the stuffing over the meat and roll up. Tie up with thread and season with a little salt on the outside.

Fry the meat well on all sides in oil preheated in a pan. Separately fry the bacon, onion and vegetables cut into small pieces, and add to the meat. Pour over a little vinegar and wine, add the bay leaf and peppercorns. Cover with aluminium foil and place into the oven preheated to 200 ° C/400 ° F/Gas 6 for about 60 minutes. When almost done take away the aluminium foil, roast a little bit more, pour over the remaining wine and water if needed.

Take out the roasted meat, remove the thread and cut into slices. Arrange them on a heated plate, pour over the puréed sauce into which you have previously mixed in the butter. Serve with potato croquettes.

Boiled Veal Knuckle

(serves 4)

Traditional

Whether made of boiled veal knuckle or lamb, this dish raises everyone's spirits. The cook who is making the complete meal in one pot by cooking together the soup, meat and vegetables, as well as those who consume this wonderful food. This very tasty and practical dish is from the Lika region, and you can find it when visiting the Plitvice Lakes in Croatia.

Ingredients:

1 veal knuckle
150 g/5 oz carrots
100 g/3 1/2 oz celeriac
1 small cabbage head
500 g/1 lb potatoes
1 tomato
peppercorns
salt
200 ml/7 fl oz dry white wine
1 bunch parsley
1 tablespoon Vegeta

Cut the meat in half and blanche shortly in boiling water. Throw away the water. Place the meat in 2 liters/7 pints of water to which you have added salt, pepper and Vegeta. Cook slowly over a moderate temperature until the meat is half tender. Add the tomato, celeriac and carrots cut into sticks, and continue cooking. After ten minutes add the potatoes cut into slices, and the cabbage cut into parts. When almost done add the wine.

Remove the cooked meat, bone it, arrange in a bowl together with the cooked vegetables, pour over the soup and sprinkle with chopped parsley.

Cooking time: about 2 hours
(One serving amounts to: 665/2795 Cal J)

Note:
You may use lamb meat to prepare this dish, but always cook the meat at a moderate temperature. The vegetables should be added gradually, so that they keep their nice form and the soup remains clear.

Pork Knuckle on the Spit

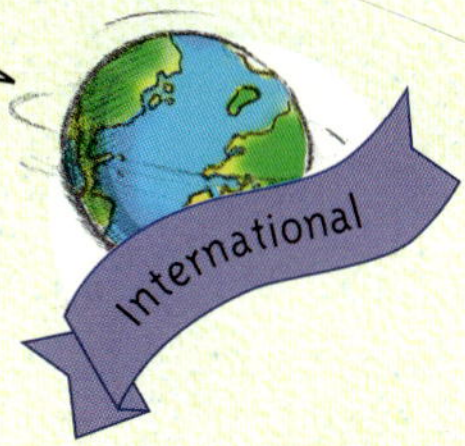

(serves 2)

To stay in Vienna and not visit the Prater Park is just like never having been there at all. To be in Prater and not taste pork knuckle cooked on a spit-fire is like never having visited Vienna no matter how many veal escalopes Vienna style you have had. Although it seems like bait for tourists, roast or boiled pork knuckle, especially if served with potatoes and cabbage, is a tasty filling dish which is conquering the world, served most often in ale bars.

Ingredients:

1 fresh pork knuckle
salt
1 tablespoon Vegeta

Season the meat well with salt and leave to rest in the refrigerator for at least one day. Cook in salty water. (The cooking time is about one hour, depending on the knuckle size). When it is half done, take out the meat, cool a little and make round deep cuts. Rub Vegeta into the cuts and place over the barbecue spit. Cook for about half an hour, until the knuckle has a golden crunchy exterior.

You can serve grated horseradish or some other garnish with this tasty simple meal which you can prepare in any season.

Note:
You can continue cooking the half-done knuckle in the oven instead over a spit-fire.

Cooking time: about 1 hour and 45 minutes plus pickling time
(One serving amounts to: 737/3095 CalJ)

Pork, veal or lamb ribs are part of traditional dishes in many national cuisines, ranging from North and South America, Germany and Austria, France and Denmark, Spain, the Caribes, Croatia, all the way to China. In the past, nutritious winter dishes always included smoked, pickled, and boiled ribs. Today fresh ribs cooked over a spit-fire or barbecued are a favorite. Vegeta's cuisine will surprise you with very tasty ribs which are often prepared in the area of the former Austrian/Hungarian Empire.

Roast Ribs with Peppers

(serves 4)

Ingredients:

11/2 kgs/5 lbs pork ribs
salt, pepper
3 tablespoons oil
2-3 red peppers
200 g/7 oz small onions
4-5 garlic cloves
2 bay leaves
3-5 juniper-berries, thyme
1 hot chilli pepper
100-150 ml/4 oz- 1/2 pint white wine
1 tablespoon Vegeta

If necessary, remove the excess fat from the ribs, season with salt, pepper and leave to rest, best overnight.

Place the ribs in an oiled tin and roast covered at 220° C/425° F/Gas 7. In the meantime clean and cut the peppers into small pieces and fry in oil. Add the small onions, chopped garlic, bay leaf, juniper-berries, thyme and chilli pepper. Sprinkle with Vegeta, pour over with wine and cook slowly. Finally add about 150 ml / 1/4 pints water.

During roasting time turn over the ribs once. When they are half-tender, arrange the prepared peppers with the small onions and spices in the baking tin. Continue cooking uncovered and add some water, if necessary.

Cut the ribs into pieces, arrange them on a plate together with the peppers, and serve with fried or baked potatoes.

Cooking time: about 1 hour and 30 minutes plus pickling time
(One serving amounts to: 976/4061 Cal J)

We can thank the shepherds from the former Pannonian flatlands for the tasty goulash, which today is the specialty of many a Budapest restaurant preparing national specialties. The Vegeta cooking team tasted it in one of the famous Czardas along the Balaton Lake. Of the many various recipes for this tasty meat dish which is made with a lot of onion and pepper, a dish which has conquered the world via Viennese cuisine, the Vegeta team presents the most unusual one - baked in the oven. Pasta or potatoes are usually served with the standard goulash, whereas our dish contains potatoes baked together with the meat.

Oven Goulash

(serves 4)

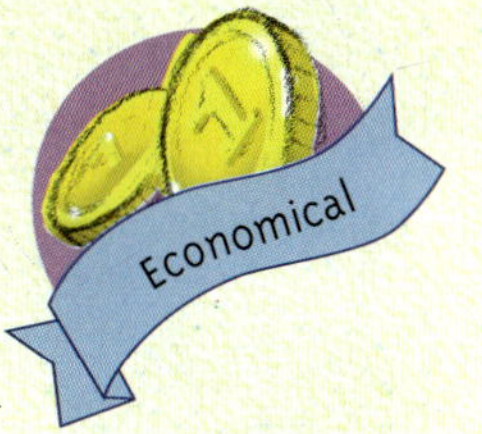

Ingredients:

600 g/1 1/4 lb beef for goulash
100 g/3 1/2 oz smoked bacon
150 g/5 oz onions
600 g/1 1/4 oz potatoes
400 g/ 14 oz fresh peppers
100 ml/4 fl oz white wine

Marinade:

5 tablespoons oil
1 teaspoon caraway seeds, salt
1 teaspoon ground red paprika
1-2 chilli peppers
3 garlic cloves
lemon rind
1 tablespoon Vegeta

Dice the meat and then prepare the marinade. Mix the oil, crushed garlic, chopped caraway seeds previously soaked, grated lemon rind, ground pepper, chopped hot pepper, salt and Vegeta.

Stir this marinade into the meat and leave to rest at least one hour, or overnight.

In the meantime slice the onions thinly, cut the peppers into biggish pieces, and the peeled potatoes into slices.

Cover the bottom of an oven-proof casserole or baking tin with bacon slices, arrange a part of the potatoes and the pepper pieces over the bacon, season with salt, add a layer of the marinated meat, and finally the onion slices. Repeat this procedure. You can pour a little oil over the surface and cover the dish firmly.

Place in an oven preheated to 220° C/ 440° F (Gas 7) and bake for about one hour and a half. After about one hour stir the ingredients carefully, pour over the wine, add a little water, cover once again and bake for approximately another half hour.

Cooking time: about 2 hours plus marinating time
(One serving amounts to: 816/3430 Cal J)

Ismir Escalopes

(serves 4)

The Turkish cuisine is based on the many products found in this region which has always been the crossroads of many civilizations, and even ordinary dishes such as minced meat escalopes can have a new, surprising taste.

Ingredients:

400 g/14 oz finely minced beef or lamb
2-3 slices of white bread
salt, pepper
2 cloves garlic
1 onion
100 ml/4 fl oz oil (olive oil and sunflower oil mixture)
parsley, origano
500 g/ 1 lb potatoes
3-4 tomatoes or 300 g/10 oz preserved chopped tomatoes
4 small green chilli peppers
1 tablespoon Vegeta

Add the soaked and drained bread to the minced meat, the grated onion and garlic, salt and pepper. Mix well all the ingredients and make small escalopes.

Slice the peeled potatoes into half a centimeter (1/4 inch) thick slices and fry in hot oil. Remove the potatoes from the frying pan, arrange in an oven-proof casserole or baking tin, season with salt. Fry the escalopes on both sides (add some more oil, if necessary), and arrange over the potatoes. Finally cook pepper rounds and peeled chopped tomatoes in the same fat. (If you do not have green chilli peppers, you can use red ones).

Add origano and Vegeta, cook briefly and pour over the escalopes. Add about 100 ml/4 fl oz water. Bake in the oven for about 20 minutes at 180 °C/350 °F/Gas 4. Decorate with parsley leaves, fried peppers and tomatoes.

Cooking time: about 45 minutes
(One serving amounts to: 670/2815 Cal J)

Born in USA and Canada, the young couple Jane Ivana Marin and Nikola Vidak who have returned to the land of their ancestors are living now in the Zagorje region town Pojatno, and like to prepare the traditional American barbecue. But not far away, on the Hušnjakovo Hill by Krapina, barbecue was perhaps something known to Grandpa Kajbumščak or Homo Crapiniensis as far back as the Paleolite.

Multi-Coloured Barbecue

(serves 10)

For picnics

Ingredients:

1 1/2 kgs/5 lbs pork (leg, loin or neck)
hot red paprika
salt
freshly ground pepper
beer
500 g/1 lb fresh peppers
500 g/1 lb onion
500 g/1 lb aubergine
oil
1 tablespoon Vegeta

Cut the meat into cubes. Cut one pepper and a little onion into strips. Arrange the meat in a bowl, sprinkle with hot red ground paprika and Vegeta. Place the prepared pepper and onion pieces between the meat pieces. Pour over the ale and leave to rest for at least 2 hours, best overnight.

Cut the peppers, onions and aubergines into biggish pieces. Drain the marinated meat well. Thread the meat and vegetables pieces alternately on skewers. Season with a little salt and pepper and brush with oil. Cook the kebabs on a well heated grill and brush with the remaining oil during grilling.

Note:
The longer the dish is marinated, the tastier it becomes, so it is best to prepare it the day before your picnic.

Cooking time: about 1 hour plus marinating time
(One serving amounts to: 501/2105 Cal J)

It may seem that everything has been said about cooking and serving smoked pork hock, but there are always surprises. Thinly sliced hock served with kale prepared in a more refined manner than the traditional stew, with a spicy sauce is an interesting (and economical) dish with a more familiar home-made taste. It can also be served on festive occasions.

Pork Knuckle New Style

(serves 4)

Ingredients:
- 1 smoked pork hock (about 1 kg/2 lbs)
- 1 kale (about 600 g/1 1/4 lb)
- 60 g/2 oz butter or margarine
- salt, freshly ground pepper
- 20 g/3/4 oz flour
- 100 ml/3 1/2 oz cream
- 2 teaspoons Estragon mustard
- marjoram
- 1 tablespoon Vegeta

Boil the washed knuckle briefly, drain the water and cook again in fresh water adding Vegeta. Leave to cook slowly over a low temperature. Remove the skin from the cooked meat, remove the bone, and cut the meat into thin slices and place in a small quantity of the hot soup.

Remove the kale leaves from the head and cut away the thick stem parts. Wash and cut into pieces about 4 cm/1 1/2 inch thick. Stew the kale pieces in 30 g/1 oz butter, pour over a cup of the soup and cook slowly for about 10 minutes. Season with salt, if necessary.

Prepare the sauce separately:

Stir the remaining flour in the heated butter, pour over 200 ml/7 fl oz hock soup and stir well. Add the cream and cook slowly for 10 minutes. When almost cooked, season with the marjoram, pepper and mustard. Arrange the meat pieces on a hot plate, as well as the stewed kale and part of the prepared sauce. Serve the remaining sauce separately. Serve this dish with boiled potatoes.

Cooking time: about 2 hours
(One serving amounts to: 923/3876 Cal J)

Note:
Pork hock should be cooked slowly over a low temperature so that it remains juicy, and so that the soup remains as tasty as possible, because it is used for pouring over the kale and making the sauce. Care should be taken that the soup is not too watery.

Dishes from the Medimurean region in northern Croatia are quite distinctive compared with other regional Croatian cooking, and one often finds combinations there of inventive rural and refined aristocratic dishes. Old records note all the fresh sea fish, spices, fruits and vegetables grown in the coastal region which were ordered by the Zrinski counts and transported to the town of Čakovec. The following wild game ragout was also inspired by dishes from Medimurje, and enjoying it is definitely not reserved only for hunters.

Wild Game Ragout

(serves about 6)

Ingredients:

1 kg/2 lbs wild game
(deer, rabbit, boar)
garlic cloves, thyme
60 g/2 oz carrots
60 g/2 oz celeriac
200 g/7 oz onion
freshly ground pepper, salt
1 tablespoon tomato pureé
bay leaves, juniper-berries, cloves
500 ml/16 fl oz red wine
4 tablespoons oil, salt
200 g/7 oz champignons/button mushrooms
20 g/3/4 oz butter
1 tablespoon Vegeta

Dice the wild game meat and place in a bowl. Sprinkle with chopped garlic, thyme and Vegeta. Pour over the wine and leave covered to marinate overnight.

Dice finely the carrots, celeriac and onions.

Drain the marinade, dry the meat with paper towels, and fry in hot oil, so that it changes colour. Add the prepared vegetables, season with pepper and salt and fry briefly.

Add the tomatoes, bay leaf, juniper-berries and cloves. Stir, pour over the marinade and enough water to cover completely the contents in the saucepan. Cook slowly with the lid on over a low heat until the meat becomes tender.

Fry the halved or quartered champignons/button mushrooms in butter, season with a little salt, add to the ragout shortly before serving the meal.

You may garnish this tasty dish with flour dumplings and juniper-berries which go well with any wild game dish.

Note:
This marinating procedure is very practical and influences significantly the taste of the cooked dish. You can prepare beef ragout in the same manner.

Cooking time: about 1 hour plus marinating time
(One serving amounts to: 408/1713 Cal J)

Wild Game Goulash

(serves 10)

Before becoming a hobby and a way to collect trophies, hunting meant survival for man. Slavko Brozović who has been taking part in hunting tourism on the southern slopes of Kapela for two decades now has equal respect for it. The following recipe is his own and he kindly gave it to the Vegeta cooking team.

Ingredients:

2 kg/4 lbs wild game meat (deer, boar)
100 ml/4 fl oz oil
1kg/2 lbs onion
50 g/1 1/2 oz smoked bacon
5 cloves garlic
250 g/9 oz carrots
150 g/5 oz celeriac root and leaves
150 g/5 oz parsley root
1 tablespoon ground hot red paprika
salt
2 pairs home-made sausages
100 - 200 ml/3 1/2 - 7 fl oz white wine
bay leaf
2 - 3 tablespoons tomato pureé
100 ml/4 fl oz sour cream
2 tablespoons Vegeta

Cut the wild game meat into biggish pieces. Fry on all sides in hot oil. Remove and keep in a closed bowl in a warm place. Fry the chopped onion, garlic, sliced carrots, parsley root, celeriac root and bacon. When the vegetables become tender return the meat to the pot, add the bay leaf, a little salt, red paprika and Vegeta. Stir all the ingredients well, fry briefly and continue cooking, adding hot water occasionally. Add the sausages. When almost cooked, and the meat has become tender, add the tomatoes, pour wine into the goulash, stir in the sour cream.

Serve polenta, bread dumplings or boiled potatoes with the goulash.

Note:
Wild game meat has to be marinated only if caught in mating time. In other periods this is not necessary for the natural aromas to be better preserved.

Cooking time: about 1 hour and 40 minutes
(One serving amounts to: 548/2302 Cal J)

Rabbit in a Pot

(serves 4)

Although quite a few people don't like it, rabbit meat is highly esteemed by nutritionists as the best meat of all. Due to its valuable ingredients the so-called white meat which is easily digested and has a small number of calories, has become part of many diets as well as of sophisticated cuisines, like the French or Italian, from where this specialty originates.

Ingredients:

1 rabbit (about 1 kg/2 lbs)

100 ml/4 fl oz wine vinegar

2 cloves garlic

1 small hot chilli pepper

1 strand of rosemary

100 ml/4 fl oz olive oil

salt, pepper

150 ml/6 fl oz dry white wine

1 tablespoon Vegeta

Cut the rabbit into pieces, dip into a mixture of water (200 ml/8 fl oz) and vinegar. Drain the meat pieces. Put the chopped chilli pepper, garlic cloves cut in halves and the rosemary into the olive oil and pour over the meat. Cover and leave in the refrigerator for at least 2 hours, best overnight.

Take out the meat and fry the garlic in the oil left after marinating. Remove the garlic from the oil, add the rabbit meat and fry well on all sides. Season with a little salt and pepper and sprinkle with Vegeta. Pour over the wine, return the rosemary and chilli pepper and stew slowly for about 40 minutes. Add small quantities of water during cooking. If you want a larger quantity of sauce, add a teaspoon of cornflour mixed in a small quantity of water.

When the meat becomes tender arrange it on a hot plate, pour over the sauce, and serve with polenta.

Cooking time: about 1 hour plus marinating time
(One serving amounts to: 630/2649 Cal J)

Electrolux offers solutions for preparing grilled dishes in your own kitchen. For this purpose you can use the grill with volcano rocks in combination with a deep-frying vessel.

Grill with deep-frying vessel
This unit is appropriate for grilling all kinds of meat, fish and poultry. Volcano rocks, after being heated with electric heaters exude the accumulated heat and give the food the aroma of real natural coal.

Note:
In case you do not have the time to wait for the fish to defrost, you can begin preparing it while still frozen. Bear in mind not to expose to too high a temperature while cooking.

fish dishes

1. Thick Fish Soup
2. Small Crab Croquettes
3. Cartoccio
4. Octopus Burgers
5. Fish Fillet with Cucumbers
6. Fish in Ale-Based Batter
7. Fish Fillets with Spaghetti
8. Scorpionfish "Beli"
9. Fish Lisabon Style
10. Fresh-Water Fish Brodetto
11. Trout English Style
12. Trout Old Salzburg Style
13. Stuffed Squid "Rivica"

fish dishes

Helene D'Arica named her restaurant "Le Bistrot des Artistes" in Nice after the famous artists, who followed such great names as Renoir, Picasso, Maupassant, Baudelaire, Tolstoy..., and spent their holidays and had their meals in the charming Provançal guest houses. Bills were usually paid with paintings, a poem or performance.

The Vegeta cooking team had great meals there, and was especially impressed by the thick fish soup of exceptional taste, always served with "Rouille" sauce.

~ Thick Fish Soup ~

(serves 4)

Traditional

Ingredients:
1 kg/2 lbs sea fish (red scorpionfish, dory, conger eel, hake)
1-2 onions
2 cloves garlic
600 g/1 1/2 lb tomatoes
ground chilli pepper
ground saffron
bunch of thyme, bay leaf and parsley
1 small glass brandy
6 tablespoons olive oil
8 thin slices French bread (baguette)
grated sheep cheese
1 tablespoon Vegeta

Rouille Sauce:
4 garlic cloves
2 egg yolks
1 teaspoon ground red chilli pepper
ground saffron
salt
250 ml/8 fl oz olive oil

Cut the cleaned fish into slices, season with salt and pepper and fry in very hot olive oil. Place in a saucepan and keep warm.

Fry the sliced onion and crushed garlic in the remaining oil. Pour over the fish. Pour the brandy into the frying pan and then add this to the fish.

Place the saucepan over a medium heat and pour over the fish 1 1/2litres/5 pints of water. Add the sliced tomatoes, saffron, Vegeta and a bunch of bay leaves, thyme and parsley leaves. Cook slowly for 1 hour.

Fry the bread slices in the meantime and make the yellow Rouille sauce:

Crush the garlic finely, add the egg yolks and make a mayonnaise, adding oil gradually. Mix in the ground hot chilli pepper, saffron and season with salt. Remove the bouquet garni. Place the cooked fish on a plate, remove the bones, press through a sieve together with the soup it was cooked in. Place back into the saucepan, add salt if necessary and season with hot chilli pepper.

When serving, place 2 slices of bread on each plate over which you have spread the prepared sauce and sprinkle with sheep cheese.

Cooking time: about 1 hour and 30 minutes
(One serving amounts to: 790/3321 Cal J)

The monuments and museums of Portugal provide proof of how great a sea force Portugal once was. But sea products play an important part on the Portugese table. Especially tasty are the excellent dishes made from fresh Atlantic fish, ranging from pilchards and cod, to salmon, gilthead and crabs.

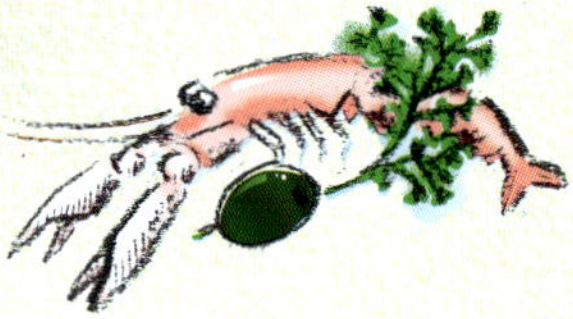

Small crab Croquettes

(serves 4)

Ingredients:

700 g/1 1/2 lb fresh small crabs (or shrimps)
800 ml/1 1/4 pints water
80 g/2 1/2 oz flour
40 g/1 1/2 oz butter
1 tablespoon breadcrumbs
2 egg yolks, pepper, salt, egg, breadcrumbs for breading
frying oil
1 tablespoon Vegeta

Add Vegeta to boiling water, then the washed shrimps, and boil slowly about 5 minutes. Then drain the liquid - soup base and leave it aside.

Clean the shrimp tails removing the shells. Cool the tails and chop finely. Place the shells back into the soup and continue cooking for 20-30 minutes. Fry the flour light golden yellow and pour over the cool soup which you have passed through a sieve (about 250 ml/8 fl oz). Continue cooking, stirring continuously, until it becomes a thick homogenous mixture. Add the shrimp tails, season with pepper, and salt to taste. Chill.

After the soup has cooled down, add the egg yolks and breadcrumbs. Make croquettes or balls from this mixture, the size of walnuts. Dip into egg mixture, then roll in breadcrumbs and fry in well heated oil until golden yellow. Place on kitchen paper towels to absorb the surplus oil.

You can serve various salads and ketchup and mayonnaise-based sauces with these tasty shrimp croquettes.

Note:
If you wish, you can fry the croquettes in an olive oil and sunflower oil mixture.

Cooking time: about 1 hour
(One serving amounts to: 415/1744 Cal J)

Millions of tourists from all over the world are impressed by Venetian restaurants, and Vegeta's cooking team could not remain indifferent. Especially after tasting the following attractive dish in Ristorante "La Colomba". It includes various seafood wrapped in parchment paper and unwrapped when ready, at the table.

Note:
Although it is best to combine several kinds of fish for this dish, you can use only one type of white fish. This attractive manner of preparation may be made more simple in the following way: instead of wrapping the fish in paper, you can arrange the contents in an oven-proof casserole, cover and bake in the oven.

Cartoccio

(serves 4)

Ingredients:
4 fresh salmon escalopes (400 g/14 oz)
4 frog-fish fillets (400 g/14 oz)
4 gilthead or sea-bass escalopes (400 g/14 oz)
4 biggish scampi
500 g/1 lb various shell-fish
salt, a little flour
100 ml/4 fl oz olive and sunflower oil mixture
basil leaves, parsley
100 g/3 1/2 oz chopped tomatoes
300 ml/ 1/2 pint brandy, 200 ml/7 fl oz white wine
green and black olives
capers, 1 tablespoon Vegeta

Clean the fish and cut into thick escalopes. Make a basic stock from the fish heads and tails. Clean the shell-fish well with a brush. Chop the parsley and basil leaves. Season the fish and scampi with salt, flour them and fry in well heated oil. Pour over the brandy, set alight and extinguish with wine. Add the chopped tomatoes, green and black olives, capers and shell-fih. Sprinkle all the ingredients with parsley, basil and Vegeta, and then pour over a small quantity of the fish stock.

You can continue cooking this dish covered in the oven or leave on the stove to cook slowly for about 8 - 10 minutes. Place a piece of parchment paper over a shallow metal platter or tin, place two smaller pieces on top of it arranging over them the

scampi, fish and other ingredients, and then pour over the sauce. Smear the edges of the large parchment paper with an egg mixture, cover the fish with it, and roll the paper edges. Use a painting brush to make a mixed egg net over the paper surface. Place everything in a hot oven and bake for 3-5 minutes at 250° C/450° F. When the paper spreads out, place the dish in front of the guests and only then cut the paper.

Cooking time: about 1 hour
(One serving amounts to: 707/2969 Cal J)

Octopus Burgers

(serves 4)

The Crikvenica riviera is well-known for its health-program tourism. The Vegeta cooking team has very pleasant memories of their impressions getting to know the gastronomic pleasures of this area. In the Amor Restaurant we were reminded of an unusual old-fashioned, but at the same time, very modern and healthy octopus dish.

Ingredients:

2 kg octopus/ 4 lbs octopus
2 eggs
2 pieces anchovy fillets
salt, pepper
3 cloves garlic
parsley
50 ml/3 fl oz olive oil
1 tablespoon breadcrumbs
frying oil
1 tablespoon Vegeta

Cook the cleaned octopus in boiling unsalted water slowly until it becomes tender. Drain, cool and mince

Add mixed eggs to the minced octopus, freshly ground pepper, fillets, chopped garlic and parsley.

Add the olive oil, breadcrumbs, some more salt to taste and Vegeta. Mix all the ingredients well and make burgers.

Fry the burgers in hot oil on both sides.

Serve boiled mangold, potatoes or courgettes with these tasty burgers.

Note:
Instead of octopus you may use squids and cuttle-fish for the burgers.

Cooking time: about 1 hour and 30 minutes
(One serving amounts to: 611/2567 Cal J)

Fish Fillets with Cucumbers

(serves 4)

Modern nutrition prescribes combining meat dishes with vegetables, especially those cooked over steam, rather than with pasta, rice or potatoes. A dish based on cucumbers prepared in a new way was revealed to us by Vlasta Brozičević, a doctor from Selce.

Ingredients:

600 g/1 1/4 lb fish fillets
3 tablespoons oil
2 tablespoons flour
1 lemon
1 kg/2 lbs cucumbers
2 cloves garlic
100 ml/4 fl oz sour cream or yogurt
2 tablespoons chopped dill
salt
freshly ground pepper
1 tablespoon Vegeta

Wash the cucumbers, peel partly and cut lengthwise. If necessary, remove the pulp and cut the cucumbers into 1 cm/1/2 inch wide pieces.

Place the cucumbers in a saucepan containing a small amount of water (2 tablespoons), add Vegeta and cook for about 10 minutes. Add the crushed garlic and chopped dill, freshly ground pepper, sour cream or yogurt. Stir all the ingredients and season with salt to taste.

In the meantime while the cucumbers are cooking, prepare the fish. Season the fish fillets with salt, dust them with flour, and fry on both sides in hot oil. Arrange them on a plate together with the prepared cucumbers and sliced lemon.

Cooking time: about 45 minutes
(One serving amounts to: 447/1878 Cal J)

Fish in Ale-Based Batter

(serves 4-6)

This very tasty, juicy and economical dish may be served as hors d'oeuvres or a main dish, and also as a light snack. It may be combined with sauces and salads. Ale-based batter can be used for frying sea and river fish, shrimps, mushrooms, cauliflower, aubergines...

Ingredients:

For the ale-based batter:

250 g/9 oz flour
200 ml/7 fl oz ale
2 eggs
2 egg whites
salt

800 g hake fillets
lemon juice
salt
freshly ground pepper
frying oil
1 teaspoon Vegeta

Cut the fish fillets into 3-4 cm/1 - 1 1/2 inch long pieces. Marinate the fish pieces with lemon juice, freshly ground pepper, salt and Vegeta.

Prepare the ale-based batter in the following manner: Mix the flour, eggs, salt and ale into a smooth batter. Cover the bowl containing the batter and leave to rest 15 - 20 minutes. Mix the batter once again and fold in the eggs whites beaten to peak stage but not too firm. The batter contains a larger quantity of egg whites than is usual, which prevents absorption of too much fat during frying.

Dry the marinated fish pieces with paper towels so that the batter can stick to the fish as closely as possible. Then dip each fish piece into the batter and fry in hot oil. When the batter turns golden and becomes crunchy, take out the fish pieces and place on absorbent paper. Serve immediately with lemon slices, home-made cream sauce or remoulade sauce and a salad of your choice.

Note:
In order for the batter to be as fluffy as possible, fold in the beaten egg whites just before frying.

Cooking time: about 45 minutes
(One serving amounts to: 427/1793 Cal J)

Sixty years after the death of the famous French cook August Escoffier, named the Tzar of Cooking, the King among Cooks and the Cook of Kings, we can visit the Museum of Gastronomy in the house where he was born in Villeneuve-Loubet-Village. The Vegeta cooking team was aware of the respect for this old master not only in his native Provence and France, but in many restaurants and hotels all over Europe as well. We were inspired by a refined recipe for spaghetti in which Escoffier combined pasta with fish, cream and truffles, a bold move at the time, but now something very commom in modern cuisines.

We chose a simple version with hake and spaghetti, and Vegeta of course.

Fish Fillets with Spaghetti

(serves 4)

Ingredients:

8 hake fillets
salt, freshly ground pepper
1-2 cloves garlic
5 tablespoons olive oil
100 ml/4 fl oz white wine,
lemon juice
140g/5 oz thin spaghetti
400 ml/14 fl oz cream
100 g/4 fl oz beech mushrooms or 20 g/3/4 oz black truffles
1 tablespoon Vegeta

Wash the fish, dry, season with salt and pepper, rub in the garlic and lemon juice, sprinkle with Vegeta.

Place in a baking tin on cold olive oil, pour over the wine and bake in the oven for about twenty minutes.

Cook the spaghetti in salty water and drain.

Pour the cream into a saucepan, add the thinly sliced beech mushrooms or coarsely grated truffles. (If you wish, you may add a few drops of truffle aroma oil).

Season the sauce with salt and cook for about 10-15 minutes until it is fully blended, and add the cooked spaghetti when the sauce is almost cooked.

Arrange the fried fish and spaghetti on a hot plate. Decorate with lemon slices.

Cooking time: about 40 minutes
(One serving amounts to: 505/2124 Cal J)

Note:
Hake fillet is readily available and is prepared often, but just a small quantity of mushrooms will give it a surprisingly new taste. Especially if you add a few drops of oil with truffle aroma. A small quantity of grated truffles turn this dish into a festive one. If you wish to make it an everyday meal, just cook the simple version.

Scorpionfish "Beli"

(serves 4)

Feruccio Hržić has joined the world-wide ecological trend on the island of Cres, in his picturesque guest house "Beli" in the 4000 year old village of the same name where tourists who arrive along the narrow road or in boats are offered simple, tasty and very healthy traditional food of the islanders, fishermen and laborers.

Ingredients:

1 kg/2 lbs red scorpionfish
1 lemon
100 ml/4 fl oz olive oil
200 ml/7 fl oz white wine
500 ml/16 fl oz water
3 cloves garlic
salt
pepper
bay leaf
rosemary
1 kg/2 lbs potatoes
1 tablespoon Vegeta

Clean the fish, wash it and sprinkle with lemon drops, and leave to rest for 1/2 hour. Season with salt and pepper.

Pour a little oil into an oven-proof casserole, put in the prepared fish and the peeled potatoes cut into biggish pieces. Bake in the oven which you have preheated to 220° C/ 425° F/ Gas 7.

In the meantime prepare the sauce: pour the remaining oil into a saucepan, add the wine, water, garlic cloves cut in halves, pepper, bay leaves, rosemary and Vegeta, and cook briefly.

When the fish and the potatoes are half baked, pour over with the prepared sauce and bake until done.

Cooking time: about 1 hour and 30 minutes
(One serving amounts to: 679/2854 Cal J)

The Portugese will manage to convince you that they love fish very much, because it swims excellently in their wonderful olive oil, and in their even more well-known Portugese wines. But it is hard to resist cold shrimps, fresh codfish in special sauce, or cured in the ocean winds and in large-grained salt and unusual spices. The following recipe was created by the Vegeta cooking team on basis of the dish it had the pleasure of tasting in Lisabon.

Fish Lisabon Style

(serves 4-6)

Ingredients:

800 g/1 1/2 lb hake fillets or cod
500 g/1 lb tomato
350 g/12 oz onion
750 g/1 lb 10 oz potato
4 cloves garlic
2 bay leaves
1 teaspoon ground sweet red paprika
a little bit of hot ground paprika
100 ml/4 fl oz olive oil
salt
freshly ground pepper
parsley
1 tablespoon Vegeta

Slice the tomatoes, onions, garlic and peeled potatoes and cut the fish fillets into biggish pieces.

Arrange the tomatoes, potatoes, onions, garlic and fish in alternate layers in a saucepan. Sprinkle the potato and fish layers with a little Vegeta, salt and pepper. Continue making the layers until you have used up all the ingredients, and let the top layer be of potatoes. Add chopped parsley, bay leaves, sprinkle with sweet and hot ground paprika, pour over 100 ml/4 fl oz water and olive oil.

Cover the saucepan and cook slowly without stirring. If necessary, shake the saucepan only. This dish is cooked when the potato turns tender.

You may serve it as an independent fish dish at various occasions in any season, and it is especially suitable on fasting days.

Note:
A special kind of dried codfish is used in Portugal for this dish whose attractiveness and tastiness bring to mind many similar dishes of people living beside the sea. If you decide to use codfish, you need to soak it in cold water first.

Cooking time: about 1 hour
(One serving amounts to: 428/1798 Cal J)

Fresh-Water Fish Brodetto

An excellent spice to dishes is historical, family and personal experience.

The Zagreb architect, Julije De Luca had ancestors who came to Ilok on the Danube from Italy, from the Mediterranean Sea and it was by the Danube that he discovered his passion for fishing and cooking. He practices his cooking in a very bold manner in his weekend cottage by Kupa river, near the Croatian/Slovenian border. This is where he created his brodetto, unusual because he uses fresh-water fish instead of sea fish. He says that the brodetto will have an even more refined taste if you add some squid, frozen ones will do.

(serves 8)

Ingredients:

2 kg/4 lbs river fish (sheatfish or carp)
3-4 onions (about 250 g/9 oz)
100 ml/4 fl oz (olive oil and sunflower oil mixture)
parsley
3-4 cloves garlic
peppercorns, salt
2 bay leaves
ground red paprika (hot or sweet)
200 ml/7 fl oz pureed tomatoes "Podravka"
200 ml/7 fl oz white wine
2 tablespoons Vegeta

Clean the fish and cut it into pieces. Chop the onions, garlic and parsley.

Place the onion in hot oil, fry briefly, immediately add a little water. Cook briefly. Add the parsley, garlic and ground red paprika (hot or sweet - to taste). Arrange the prepared fish, season with salt and sprinkle with Vegeta. Pour over the pureed tomatoes, wine and enough water to cover the fish. Add the bay leaf, peppercorns and cook slowly for about one more hour.

Serve cooked broad macaroni or polenta with this excellent brodetto.

Note:
The fine taste, aroma and thickness needed for a really good brodetto are obtained by cooking the dish slowly over a low heat for enough time.

Cooking time: about 1 hour and 30 minutes
(One serving amounts to: 566/2380 Cal J)

184

When Vegeta established itself in the cuisines of many countries, cooks started using it in preparing traditional dishes. When the English seasoned their traditional simple fish dish with Vegeta, the common conclusion was that the recipe was too good not to include it among the selected Vegeta recipes. It will prove to be a refreshing innovation for the traditionally light Christmas Eve supper.

Cooking time: about 45 minutes
(One serving amounts to: 506/2127 Cal J)

Trout English Style

(serves 4)

Ingredients:

4 trout
100 g/2 1/2 oz butter
50 g/1 1/2 breadcrumbs
juice of one lemon
salt, parsley, chives
1 tablespoon Vegeta

Clean the trout, wash them, dry with paper towels, season with salt. Mix the Vegeta with the lemon juice and rub this mixture into the fish inside and outside. Place the trout in an oven-proof casserole greased with butter, pour in 50 ml/3 fl oz water and sprinkle with chopped chives. Cook in a preheated oven covered with aluminium foil for 20 to 25 minutes at 200°-220°C/400°-425° F/ Gas 6-7.

In the meantime briefly fry the breadcrumbs in the remaining butter, and pour them over the almost cooked fish. Return to the oven for a short time. Sprinkle with chopped parsley, decorate with lemon and serve with boiled potatoes.

Note:
If you wish you may add sour cream together with the butter and bread crumb mixture and bake in the oven for a short time. This will make this tasty and interesting dish even more rich.

Cooking time: about 45 minutes
(One serving amounts to: 518/2165 Cal J)

Trout Old-Salzburg Style

(serves 4)

In the year of Mozart's anniversary many events were organized all over the world to honor the great composer. The Salzburg cuisine recipes from Mozart's period were demonstrated throughout one whole month in the Bistro of the Zagreb Hotel "Esplanade". One of the recipes was presented by Mario Starman, who recommended it for festive occasions.

Ingredients:

4 small trouts
40 g/1 1/3 oz butter
1 onion
100 ml/4 fl oz white wine
100 ml/4 fl oz sour cream
200 ml/7 fl oz cream
salt, white pepper
1 teaspoon saffron
1 lemon

For the breading:

flour
2 eggs
corn flour
frying oil
2 teaspoons Vegeta

Make fillets out of the trout by separating the meat along the spine-bone with a sharp knife. Sprinkle with Vegeta and lemon drops. Season with salt to taste. While the trout is marinating prepare the sauce:

Fry the onion in oil until light golden, pour over the wine, let the wine evaporate and add a mixture of fresh and sour cream, salt, white pepper and a teaspoon of Vegeta. Let the sauce cook slowly until it reduces in quantity. Pass the cooked sauce through a sieve, add the remaining butter and a teaspoon of saffron. Cook briefly.

Flour the marinated trout fillets, dip them in mixed eggs and finally in cornflour. Fry in hot oil.

Arrange the fried trout on heated plates, two pieces on each, serve with vegetables and the prepared saffron sauce. Decorate with lemon slices, a stem of dill or parsley and serve.

Stuffed Squid "Rivica"

(serves 4)

The "Rivica" Res-aurant from the town of Njivice on the island of Krk has been awarded the 'Maison de qualite Saint Fortunat" Diploma, pla-ing the island on the Culi-iary map of Europe. One of Ivica Lesić's recipes vhich is based on squid is orepared in a new manner. It is a favorite dish in the iorthern Quarner Bay irea, and is sure to be ap-oreciated everywhere.

Ingredients:

1 kg/2 lbs middle-sized squid
100 g/3 1/2 oz prosciutto
250 g/9 oz red radicchio
2-3 cloves garlic
parsley
freshly ground pepper
100 ml/4 fl oz oil (olive oil and sunflower oil mixture)
1 teaspoon Vegeta

Clean the squid and prepare the stuffing: chop the tentacles and prosciutto finely, add the red radicchio cut into thin short strips, the chopped parsley and garlic. Season with ground pepper and Vegeta and stir all the ingredients well. Stuff the squid with this mixture, and close the openings with tooth picks.

Arrange the squid in a pan placing them in cold oil, cover and slowly fry first on one and then on the other side for about 15 - 20 minutes.

Serve fried potato pieces with the fried squid, or any sort of leafy salad.

Cooking time: about 35 minutes
(One serving amounts to: 479/2013 Cal J)

Note:
You can widen the natural squid openings with a small cut so that you fill them more easily.

Contents

MEAT DISHES

FISH DISHES

CIP - Katalogizacija u publikaciji
Nacionalna i sveučilišna knjižnica, Zagreb

UDK 641. 55 (083.12)

BILUŠ, Ivanka
Cooking around the world with Vegeta / Ivanka Biluš, Cirila Rodé, Božica Brkan; [food photography Davor Marjanović; English translation Dunja Knebl], - Zagreb: Alfa; Koprivnica: Podravka, 1999. - 192. str.: ilustr u bojama; 21 cm

Izv. stv. nasl.: Recepti iz Vegetine kuhinje.

ISBN 953 168 218.6 (Alfa)

1. Rodé, Cirila 2. Brkan, Božica

990915110